MAY 2010

RAISING YOUR
TODDLER

KNACK

RAISING YOUR
TODDLER

A Complete Illustrated Guide from First Steps to Preschool

MARSHA GREENBERG, LMSW, CGE

Photographs by Sue Barr

KNACK
MAKE IT EASY

Guilford, Connecticut
An imprint of Globe Pequot Press

To buy books in quantity for corporate use
or incentives, call **(800) 962–0973**
or e-mail **premiums@GlobePequot.com.**

Editor in Chief: Maureen Graney
Editor: Imee Curiel
Cover Design: Paul Beatrice, Bret Kerr
Text Design: Paul Beatrice
Layout: Joanna Beyer
Cover and interior photos by Sue Barr
Edited by Amy Wilensky

Library of Congress Cataloging-in-Publication Data

Greenberg, Marsha.
  Knack raising your toddler : a complete illustrated guide from first steps to preschool / Marsha Greenberg ; photographs by Sue Barr.
     p. cm.
  Includes index.
  ISBN 978-1-59921-620-1
  1. Toddlers. 2. Preschool children. 3. Child rearing. 4. Parenting. I. Barr, Sue. II. Title.

HQ774.5.G745 2010
649'.122—dc22
                                              2009032191

The following manufacturers/names appearing in *Knack Raising Your Toddler* are trademarks:
Band-Aid®, Benadryl®, Cheerios®, EpiPen®, iPod®, Jell-O®, Popsicle®, Tylenol®, Ziploc®

Printed in China

10 9 8 7 6 5 4 3 2 1

To my amazing sons, Josh, Noah, and Jonah, who taught me to never give up; to my wonderful grandchildren, Ethan and Graham, who taught me how to really enjoy parenting; and to my daughters-in-law, Jen, Ingrid, and Cris, who taught me how to be a stronger woman. —Marsha

Acknowledgments

I would like to say how thankful and appreciative I am to the editor of this book, Amy Wilensky, for her calming and excellent help. I also thank Sue Barr for the beautiful images that helped capture toddler behavior.

There are many people in my life who have guided and supported me, not just with this book but throughout my life as a parent and professional, including Michael Kaplan, who has shared with me his great wisdom about people of all ages; Sue Gall, my closest colleague and friend, who has been in the trenches with toddlers; Dr. James Plunket, who has taught me so much about healthy attachment; Doug Davies, who has always inspired my work with children; Janeen Hayward, who helps toddler parents every day; and Gus B. Greenberg, who has always had faith in me.

I would also like to thank my nephew Randy for his gracious assistance on the technological end of this project and Dr. C. W. Ross for reviewing the medical information. Finally, I would like to thank My Monday Mothers' Group—Georgia, Jess, Nicole, Janice, and their terrific toddlers—and all the families that allowed us to photograph their day-to-day worlds.

—Marsha Greenberg

Special thanks to Red Bank YMCA, NY A-Ha! Learning Partners, A Child Grows, River Road Books, Shore Pediatric Dental, and Marsha's Toddler Group.

Thanks to Elisha Jacobsen, Ashley Moran, Ryan Struck, and Saori Mizuguchi for keeping me covered, organized, and directed, and to Marsha Greenberg for teaching me toddler basics.

Thank you to all the wonderful families that participated in the many photo shoots, especially the Avery Family, Chakrapani Family, Daniels Family, DiPiero Family, Edwards Family, Gordon Family, Grillo Family, Hussey Family, Karan Family, Ketchow Family, Leffe Family, Mallach Family, Pasmore Family, Reid Family, Robinson Family, Savko Family, Segall Family, Spellame Family, Streberger Family, Thomases Family, Valerio Family, Verrone Family, and Witt Family.

But especially thanks to my son, Jake, and Elisha's husband, Dusty, for all your patience, laying low, and just letting us do our thing.

—Sue Barr

CONTENTS

Introduction viii

Chapter 1: Who Is Your Toddler?
Becoming a Toddler xii
Temperament & Mood 2
Persistence & Adaptability 4
Regularity & Activity 6
Parental Attitudes 8
Birth Order 10

Chapter 2: 12 to 18 Months: Milestones
Cognitive Development 12
Physical Development 14
Emotional Development 16
Social Development 18
Language Development 20
Self-Esteem 22

Chapter 3: 12 to 18 Months: Care
Schedules & Routines 24
Toddlers & Sleep 26
Keeping Toddlers Safe 28
Toddlers & Teeth 30
Your Toddler's Health 32
Preparing for a Trip 34

Chapter 4: 12 to 18 Months: Meals
Toddlers & Food 36
Transitioning to Table Food 38
Is Food So Important? 40
Toddler Eating Habits 42
Family Mealtime 44
Allergies 46

Chapter 5: 12 to 18 Months: Play
Importance of Play 48
Solitary Play 50
Importance of Toys 52
Play Spaces 54
Great Toddler Books 56
Playing with Your Toddler 58

Chapter 6: 12 to 18 Months: Socializing
Learning to Socialize 60
Toddler Socialization 62
Separation: Painful & Important 64
Pregnancy & Toddlers 66
Encouraging Friendships 68
Special Outings 70

Chapter 7: 18 to 24 Months: Milestones
Cognitive Development 72
Physical Development 74
Emotional Awareness 76
Social Milestones 78
Language Grows Quickly 80
Further Developing Self-Esteem 82

Chapter 8: 18 to 24 Months: Care
Supporting Independence 84
Changing Sleep Routines 86
An Exciting & Dangerous World 88
Visiting the Dentist 90
Doctor Visits 92
Preparing for Travel 94

Chapter 9: 18 to 24 Months: Meals
Feeding a Toddler 96
More on the Floor 98
Where Did My Bottle Go? 100
Hunger Strikes 102
Family Times Still Important 104
Food Allergies 106

Chapter 10: 18 to 24 Months: Play
Toddler Play Is Changing 108
Parallel Play 110
Toys, Toys, Toys 112
Books Open New Worlds 114
Play Is Hard Work 116
Parents Play Differently 118

Chapter 11: 18 to 24 Months: Socializing
Toddlers Really Do Connect 120
Group Think 122
Helping Toddlers Play 124
Hellos & Good-Byes 126
Toddler Talk 128
Pregnancy & Toddlers 130

Chapter 12: 24 to 36 Months: Milestones
Cognitive Development 132
Moving with Purpose 134
Big Feelings 136
High Society 138
Toddlers Say a Lot 140
Mirroring Healthy Confidence 142

Chapter 13: 24 to 36 Months: Care
Sleep Challenges 144
Safety for Adventurous Toddlers 146
Preventing Tooth Decay 148
Healthy Checkups & Checklists 150
Traveling with Older Toddlers 152

Chapter 14: 24 to 36 Months: Meals
Toddlers & Mealtime 154
Manners 156
Fussy Eaters 158
Family Mealtimes 160
Birthdays & Allergies 162
Gardening with Toddlers 164

Chapter 15: 24 to 36 Months: Play
Experiences & the Brain 166
Dramatic Play 168
Flexible Toys 170
Books & More 172
How to Play 174
Art, Music & Dance 176

Chapter 16: 24 to 36 Months: Socializing
Friends & Family 178
Too Much Stimulation 180
Preparing for School 182
Groups of Toddlers 184
Separation Anxiety 186
Bringing a New Baby Home 188
Toddler Friendships with Peers 190

Chapter 17: Potty Training
Potty Training Readiness 192
Parents' Role in Potty Training 194
Practice Doesn't Make Perfect 196
To Reward or Not 198
Equipment for Toilet Training 200
Saying Good-Bye to Diapers 202

Chapter 18: Behavior & Discipline
Age-Appropriate Guidelines 204
Understanding Toddler Emotions 206
Talking to Your Toddler 208
Temper Tantrums 210
Which Battles to Tackle? 212
Keeping Your Feelings in Check 214

Chapter 19: Everyday Family Life
Time to Yourself 216
Time for Partners 218
Media Exposure 220
Cleanup Times 222
Managing Your Time 224
Creating Family Rituals 226

Chapter 20: Resource Directory
Resources 228
Glossary 235
Index 237

INTRODUCTION

This book is a compilation of my experiences, both professional—as an educator and therapist—and personal—as a parent and grandparent. There is so much to say about toddlers, but a toddler does not exist in a vacuum, so I had to write about family and systems and how we grow and develop as people, too, when we are parenting. As parents or grandparents, we barely have time to keep up with our daily lives, let alone the constant flow of information regarding child development. It is reassuring, though, to know for certain that both nature and nurture play a significant role

in who our children are and how they cope with the world.

Human development is not simple. Because of the rapid advances in the field of neuroscience, we know much more than we used to, but we are still hypothesizing. We now know that the brain is more malleable than previously thought and can be shaped and reshaped through positive experiences with our children. We have always known that we cannot prevent bad, sad, confusing, or upsetting things from happening to our children, but we also now know that we can help children learn how to manage their feelings

problem solver requires opportunities for experimentation in a safe environment; becoming responsible takes seeing others modeling responsibility.

I remember reading a parenting book shortly after my first son turned two and thinking, "Oh, no. I have already messed this up." Sometimes I had. But parenting is an art influenced by science, practicality, and our life experience. Trying our best, whatever that is in the moment, makes for good enough parenting most of the time. When things go awry—and they will—parents can think about what they will do next time, because there is almost always a next

and frame their experiences in ways that do not jeopardize their self-esteem and self-worth.

All children are born with strong impulses. It is that kind of aggressive stirring that helps them survive, but helping toddlers know when and how to use that aggression and how to do it in ways that are mindful of others is one of the hardest parts of parenting. It is sometimes easier for us to lash out in the moment when we are frustrated, but when we do, that lashing out becomes the toddler's take-away. Becoming empathic is a learning process; becoming a time. Guilt can be instructive, but shame never is, so when you think you have fallen short, let your feelings guide you to a better way as you move on. Beating yourself up compounds whatever mistakes you think you have made with your children. Perfection is not a human quality, and we need to use this as a guiding principle in our parenting.

I have had many opportunities professionally to work with families and have brought the insights and dilemmas of new parents to the material I have presented here. I will give you the backstory of what is happening developmentally so you can try to make sense of your own toddler's development. I have taught childbirth education classes

for nearly 35 years and have listened to parents talk about their hopes and fears of giving birth and transitioning to becoming parents. Never before have we understood the impact of becoming a family the way we do now in the face of so many divorces. When you become a parent, you become part of a family in a different way than ever before.

As a working parent myself and as the director of Group 243's first on-site workplace child-care system, the first in southeast Michigan, and later as the director of the University of Michigan Health System Child Care System, I had the opportunity to work closely with working parents. I have held their toddlers while the parents struggled to separate from them to go to work each day, to balance their needs as parents and professionals. I currently facilitate mothers' groups for infants and toddlers in New York City and see every day how parents work to do the best they can for their children, even when resources like time, money, or energy are compromised.

As a social worker, I have seen how our own early experiences impact our parenting. We can feel our emotions spin out of control so quickly that to be responsible for how our toddlers are feeling can overwhelm us. One of my most insightful experiences has been my recent work with families of special needs children, seeing what struggles children and families have when development is not typical.

I have tried to use all of my training and experiences as a lens for you to understand your toddler in ways that are practical and insightful. At each point in the book you need to weigh in and see where you and your child are on the continuum of development. Each family's trajectory for growth looks and feels different.

As much as we professionals sometimes sound like we know it all, never underestimate the insights and understanding you have as a parent. You are the one who knows your child best. You can tell a pediatrician or parenting-group moderator stories, but we get snapshots. You live in the documentary. I have tried to focus on the basic ways toddlers think, learn, and feel, and give you ways to problem-

solve what you are seeing with your toddler in a quick and easy format.

Perhaps the most important thing to remember is that you get to start over each day. Toddlers are pretty forgiving and will for the most part roll with the punches as we try to figure out what to do. This book is a jumping-off point, a way to move farther down the road of parenting. This time in your life goes quickly, so do your best to stay in the here and now. You cannot change the past or predict the future, but you do have the present. Use it!

—Marsha Greenberg
www.marshagreenberg.com

BECOMING A TODDLER

The move into toddlerhood is marked by many things, including the ability to motor around on two feet

Becoming a toddler is messy and complicated. After 12 months of being protected, nurtured, and fully dependent on us, babies are ready to enter their world in much more interactive ways. They are increasingly aware that they can impact the world but have no idea how it actually works. They look to their parents to explain, coach, comfort, and let go of them all at the same time. During their next 24 months, toddlers achieve significant accomplishments in the areas of movement, language, and emotion, but the interaction of these complex developmental goals is hard to predict. Toddlers and parents approach the dance of childhood with highly individual expectations and behaviors.

New Walkers

- When toddlers start to experience getting up on two feet, they will delight in walking with you. They will try over and over again to master this new skill.

- Try giving your toddler walking experiences without her shoes on to increase stability and balance.

- This is an exciting time for parents and toddlers, the opening of new worlds your toddler can access herself.

Signs of Independence

- Once toddlers have some stability on their feet, they may insist on letting go of your hand.

- With their newfound awareness of the larger world, they will take steps away and fall. It takes time for them to walk, stop, and turn around.

- Toddlers fall frequently, so pushing back tables and covering sharp edges may be required to keep things safe.

Toddlers are naturally scientific. They understand by experimenting and are not yet wired to accept limits, complicating the job of parents to keep them safe and secure. Knowing when to let toddlers explore and when to move them closer can be exhausting and exciting at the same time. We watch with pride as toddlers master walking and are worn out when they will not sit still. We are thrilled when they say "mama" and "dada" and frustrated by their constant "no." During this next stage of development, our toddlers are questioning, resisting, and changing our plans and strategies each and every day.

GREEN ● LIGHT

On your baby's first birthday, take five minutes to remember a time when you were so curious about something you could not contain your enthusiasm and excitement. Use this image to remind yourself that as the next year unfolds, it will not be just about your baby's eating and sleeping but about exploring her world. Picturing the next step of your child's development can help you determine how to manage your own emotions.

Tilting Forward

- When toddlers have finally mastered walking, they move on pretty quickly to walking and running on their own.

- Their bodies lean forward, so they are prone to losing their balance, especially on harder surfaces.

- You won't be able to protect your toddler from everything, but try to spot-check areas he will be walking on for uneven surfaces or small things he may trip over.

Opening Worlds

- Walking is the gateway for the next steps of toddler independence.

- They thrill at their ability to move away from or toward what they want to see or avoid, and begin to use movement to express their pleasure or frustration by insisting on being put down or picked up as they experiment with traveling around outside.

- Young toddlers are not aware of how they will fit in the world around them but have an increased interest in engaging in what they see.

TEMPERAMENT & MOOD

Regulating our moods is a combination of adaptability and brain wiring

Temperamental qualities do not define us but are part of the way we look at the world. As our babies enter toddlerhood, we gain a much better sense of how they are responding to routines, transitions, and new situations. Our children's temperaments can be very different from our own, making it harder for us to understand what they are experiencing,

especially before they have language. As we learn more about our toddlers' temperaments, we can begin to provide ways for them to develop strategies for managing their emotions when they boil over.

Temperamental qualities are on a continuum from a little to a lot. All children struggle with big feelings, and some need

Temperament

Temperamental qualities are not fixed at birth and can change over time, but understanding how we are predisposed can help us find our hot buttons. Make a list of adjectives that describe you, your partner, and your toddler based on the following topics:

- Tendency to move away or withdraw from new situations

- Level of anger or frustration when needs are not met

- Amount of positive emotion you/your toddler reflects

- Activity level with regard to physical movement and energy

- Attention span/ability to focus and maintain interest

- Predictable reactions to daily routines

Changing Feelings

- For toddlers happiness can change to frustration and back again in a matter of seconds.

- Some toddlers can adapt to their changing moods more quickly than others.

- Think about the list you created describing your

and your toddler's temperaments. How do they match up? Understanding how your temperaments align (or don't) and making adjustments are part of creating a positive emotional climate.

2

extra help getting steady again. Toddlers begin to display more moods as they explore more of the world. A toddler who cries every time he drops a toy needs help managing his feelings, not just retrieving the toy. Some toddlers react very strongly to everything, but this intensity in mood should not define them. We need to help them become more adaptive. Our work as parents is to help our toddlers develop more tolerance for their feelings and to deemphasize the particulars of a situation that trigger a reaction. Parents can model feelings effectively.

· · · · · · · · · · GREEN ● LIGHT · · · · · · · · · ·

When you see your toddler expressing frustration, say, "You are so angry and upset right now. You will feel better soon. I love you." Wait a minute, and repeat if needed, offering reassurance and a hug or a kiss. Your ability to offer a calming, understanding presence will help your toddler find steady ground regardless of the trigger situation.

Strong Reactions

- Toddlers can be persistent. Our job is to help them understand their frustration and to redirect them.

- They take different amounts of time to transition from feelings that they experience more intensely.

- Some toddlers will accept limits faster than others. It can take time, but they will become more comfortable accepting the limits you set.

- You may have to redirect your toddler from an unsafe behavior (like touching a light) 50 times before she is able to accept it.

Safe Spaces

- Keeping environments toddler-friendly can cut down on the number of times you have to set limits.

- Even after they seem to understand that something is dangerous, toddlers will still on occasion take risks, so be watchful.

- You never know when or where your toddler will try to experiment with a limit. It will take time to really know when you can trust your child's judgment.

PERSISTENCE & ADAPTABILITY

Toddlers persist in order to understand how the world works

Adaptability is a skill that can be learned. Humans are very adaptive, sometimes out of necessity and sometimes because we learn that it enhances our experience of the world. Adapting, however, is a huge task for toddlers. At 12 to 24 months of age, toddlers have no understanding that other people experience emotions. They are still the center of their world, and it is not until almost age three that this awareness changes, leading to empathy. Toddlers learn to manage their feelings by observing us manage ours.

One of the most difficult and important temperamental attributes toddlers struggle with is persistence. Some will let you put them in their stroller without a peep, and others will insist on pushing it along the sidewalk themselves no matter how many times they trip over the wheels. When we have a

Toddler Persistence

- Persistence is a needed attribute in life.

- Persistence is what helps toddlers stay motivated and energized to learn new skills.

- Be ready to help your toddler when persistence gives way to frustration or anger.

- Your toddler may be more persistent than you are. Temperament is not hereditary, so try to make room for your toddler's behavior.

Gaining Mastery

- Toddler attention spans at this age are still short.

- They will play for longer periods when you engage with them, especially if it is quieter play.

- Toddlers love to move, so they can insist on pushing their stroller or running ahead while you follow behind. They are practicing independence and gaining a sense of accomplishment from their physical mastery.

sense of how intensely a toddler will persist, we can move in to help with limits. Toddlers need to know we are there to help them with their feelings, even if they have a meltdown. Very persistent toddlers will be in daily situations where they become frustrated by their inability to do whatever it is they have set out to do. Modeling a calm reaction will help a toddler slow down escalating feelings.

Unpredictability

- Toddler moods can switch quickly and at times unpredictably. A toddler can be sitting peacefully in the grocery cart and minutes later be yelling and clamoring to get down.

- These can be frustrating times for parents as you try to keep your toddler engaged. Try talking to him and engaging his imagination and sense of humor. Offer an alternative interaction that will be satisfying while you get through the checkout line.

New Fears

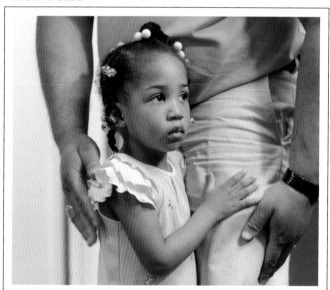

- Toddler fears are real. It is important to not over- or underreact when your child expresses worry or fear.

- She will be watching you, and if you are frustrated or short with her, it adds to her distress over the original thing that triggered the fear.

- Say to your toddler, "I think you are feeling afraid. That dog is big and noisy. Let's stand here together and see if you feel better."

REGULARITY & ACTIVITY

Each toddler reacts differently to the pace of his inner body and the activity around him

Some toddlers zip around, while others watch and wait. Each toddler has his own way of navigating his world. There is no "typical toddler"—they are as varied as adults in every way—but understanding how your toddler experiences his day can provide invaluable insight to you as a parent. You can learn by watching when your toddler needs help to be adaptive.

A toddler who is really active may have a hard time slowing down for bedtime. One who is cautious and careful may have a difficult time going on a playdate. Both toddlers can be adaptive but need very different things from us as parents.

A toddler's temperament also sheds light on how she will manage sleep schedules, eating, and transitions. Some

Naps Vary

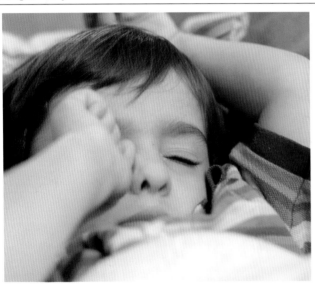

- Toddlers require 12 to 13 hours of sleep a day, including naps.

- This can vary depending on your toddler's temperament. Some will catnap during the day, and others will sleep the afternoon away.

- Over time you will get a sense of your child's daily rhythm and patterns so you can pace yourself.

- Keep a log for a week or two so you can see more clearly where you may need to shift your toddler's routine.

Eating Patterns

- How much food and the variety of foods your child will try are factors of temperament.

- Try to unhook from the notion that your child is eating too much or too little. If you offer food, she will take what she needs.

- For really active toddlers, packing a higher protein snack or shake when you are out can help avoid meltdowns.

toddlers have a more difficult time learning how to sleep through the night and need more frequent interventions to support them. This does not mean your toddler is not adaptive; it just means she needs more practice in this area. It is very important to remember that it is not how long it takes for a child to learn something, it is the way we assist her as she learns that will build temperamental flexibility and invaluable self-confidence.

········ GREEN ● LIGHT ········

Say to a toddler who is clinging to your side, "This will get easier. Watching is fine, and when you are ready I will help you move around the room." This may sound like a lot of words, but you are modeling tone and intention and sending a message to your toddler that you are there to help, at the pace that feels right for him.

Activity Levels

- Toddlers have a broad range of activity levels. Some are happy to sit and learn from watching the world, while others learn better when they are moving and actively engaged.

- Activity levels are not gender based, but the type of activities your toddler chooses is somewhat influenced by gender because of the order of muscle dexterity. As development continues, you will see that the larger muscles develop more quickly in boys and small motor muscles develop more quickly in girls.

Independence Grows

- During the second year of their lives, toddlers are trying to master a certain level of independence.

- Toddlers can be anxious when they separate from you, or bold, at least in the moment. Every toddler, no matter where he is temperamentally, looks back when you leave and has to manage his emotions.

7

PARENTAL ATTITUDES

How we interact with our toddlers impacts how they develop emotional and social skills

The role that parents play in raising children who can manage their feelings is significant. Yet most of us are just beginning to figure out our own emotions when we become parents ourselves. The doubly complicated task of parenting ourselves while we parent our children requires many things, but most of all kindness. When we do the best we can, even when it looks sloppy and we have regrets, we must take comfort in having done what we could in the moment. Perfect parenting is not possible; it is not even definable. What we can do, regardless of our parenting values, is have a willingness to change our own behaviors when what we are doing is not working.

A Good-Enough Fit

- Aligning your temperament to your toddler's takes time.

- The goal of fitting in with your toddler's temperament is to determine where frustration for each of you becomes overwhelming and try to find a good-enough balance.

- You won't always be attuned to your toddler's needs—doing the best you can is usually good enough.

- Keep looking to understand how your toddler is making sense of her world. This gives you lots of clues to where and how she can get off track.

Parent Feelings

- Parental emotions heat up at times and can be difficult to manage. Knowing your own frustration triggers is important.

- Too little sleep and not eating well can contribute to emotional fatigue.

- You may not be able to change everything in your life, but you can take small steps toward better self-care. Drink more water, surround yourself with nonjudgmental friends, and remind yourself that this time is limited.

The next time—and there usually is a next time with toddler challenges—pay attention to how your behavior is triggered by your own strong feelings. If you can determine those behaviors on the part of your toddler that trigger the strongest reactions in you, you can prepare yourself and work extra hard to keep your own feelings from escalating. Toddlers look to us to "reboot" after a hard time. When we are struggling, children take a backseat to our feelings, and it can take them twice as long to recover from an upsetting experience or meltdown.

Controlling Your Emotions

- Containing extreme emotional reactions during frustrating situations can be very hard to do but is worth the effort. This is the model of behavior your child is observing and will be most likely to repeat.

- If you are completely overwhelmed, move away, go into the bathroom, turn on the shower, and yell for a while. When you calm down, think of what you can do the next time to avoid the same situation.

Staying Present

- It is important to stay present with your toddler in an emotional way. When we are distracted, toddlers tend to react in a more challenging way.

- Remember that your toddler needs help learning the skill of waiting. It is not automatic. Give her a few books to look at and tell her that when she is done, you will be through with what you are doing. You are helping her understand competing needs.

BIRTH ORDER

Where your toddler was born in your family plays a role in how she understands the world

About 80 percent of children have siblings, and where your toddler falls in the family birth order has some impact on her behavior. Regardless of when or how a baby comes into your home, the arrival will impact your family dynamic. Greeting a new sibling is a significant adjustment for any child and can be very hard on a toddler. Feelings of jealousy and aggression are difficult to contain and are expressed at different times and in different ways. It is important to remember that sibling relationships change as children move through different developmental stages. There are many factors that influence how siblings interact, including the temperament of each child, how parents react to discord, and other life events such as divorce or job loss.

Transition to Parenting

- The first child holds a unique place in the family. It is through this birth that you begin to understand the depth of emotion that comes with parenting.

- You move through developmental stages with a mix of excitement and worry based on what is still a great unknown.

- You protect your child from the world because you are still very unsure of what she can do on her own.

Different Reactions

- Second children come into the world already knowing the voice of their bigger sibling from their time in utero. They have never known the experience of being the only one.

- When your toddler is the second, his reaction may be stronger or less intense as he waits for a turn or for your time.

- Some of the ways the second child reacts have to do with how you make room for him emotionally in the family.

The first child in a family brings our fantasies of having children and the reality of having children into direct conflict. As we work through each stage of parenting, we gain skills and learn shortcuts that can be helpful but can also lock us into behaviors that may not be ideal for our second child. Each child in a family is different, and it is essential to retool our responses—however deeply ingrained—to meet the needs of each individual child.

MAKE IT EASY

Ways to help reduce rivalry: Comfort the child that has been hurt and remind the older child that his sibling will eventually learn to use words and to share. Treat playroom toys as community property. When your toddler is jealous of the new baby, say, "I know it is hard to wait for me. Let's sing a song together while you wait."

Older Siblings

- Older children have a different developmental understanding when a baby comes into the family.

- If there is a five- or six-year difference, older children have some experience to draw on from friends or other family members.

- Older children can be very helpful, but it is important to not let them become the parent.

- Be careful to find a balance between letting them help with the baby and maintaining their own activities.

Maintaining Balance

- When toddlers have more than one older sibling, they may attach to the eldest one more quickly. This happens in part because the eldest child can be more sympathetic and also often gets kudos from adults for care and empathy.

- Balancing all your children's needs is important, so you should help to minimize sibling pairing off and leaving out the middle child.

COGNITIVE DEVELOPMENT

Toddlers are learning how to think and problem-solve as quickly as they are learning how to move

Toddler development happens in multiple ways. They learn how to walk, so they can walk to the ball and bring it to you on demand. They try to say "ball," smile, and run away from you. Toddlers are developing intelligence and cognitive awareness. Developmental milestones are being practiced, reached, perfected, and advanced. They are also developing their skills with a background of parental interest and acknowledgement. They look to us to see how they are doing and to give their experience words and shape.

Toddlers between 12 and 18 months become very interested in cause and effect. They can see that a switch turned makes a light go on, and notice how we respond to their

Cognitive Development

- Intense interest in the world around them

- Purposeful tasks—putting objects in a bucket, holding a toy phone to an ear

- Increased and demonstrated memory—remembering the location of missing objects

- Experimentation with objects—dropping spoon off high chair, throwing spoon off high chair

- Expectations of rituals—knows routines ahead of time

Developing Intelligence

- Toddlers use their developing intelligence to learn how things work. They can spend minutes dumping and filling the same container. Each time they are learning what happens and how to change or influence it.

- Point out to your toddler what you see her doing. She will use your reflecting language as another way to understand how the world works.

play and exploration. They practice anticipating and predicting what comes next, which can be gratifying or, if things don't go as expected, frustrating.

This new level of thinking can lead to increased persistence or worry in unfamiliar situations. A different sitter or a change in location can catch toddlers off guard. A toddler can stand at a baby gate and scream and scream because she now knows the excitement of stair climbing that lies on the other side. Having to redirect a young toddler to a new area of focus is a daily exercise for parents.

MAKE IT EASY

When you redirect a toddler, try to move him to another interesting area. If he wants to climb on the couch, pile up pillows on the floor, or use cardboard blocks for him to stand on. Match the redirection to a place and activity that will provide novelty as well as an equal skill challenge. This may also mean that you will need to stay more engaged in play with your toddler until he is on to something else.

Seeing Patterns

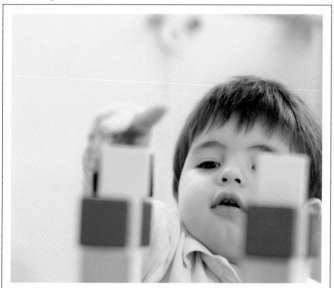

- Toddlers build at first to knock down. They are fascinated by trying to balance one block on top of another.

- Block building is an important skill in many ways. It helps toddlers understand size and shape relationships, patterns, and creativity.

- Your toddler may need help at first seeing you build a road or a building, but he will get the hang of it if the materials are around. It is best to start off with larger blocks.

Experimentation

- Toddlers love puzzles, especially with knobs for easy handling. At first they will take out the pieces and taste them.

- Sit down next to your toddler and take out a piece and put it back in a few times. He will watch and begin to model very quickly. Try not to correct at the beginning—just encourage.

- Point out what you are seeing him do. Say things like, "You are really trying to turn that piece around to help it fit in!"

PHYSICAL DEVELOPMENT

Learning how to walk and run takes practice and persistence on the part of your toddler

Physical development progresses in stages. As soon as a toddler masters one task, he is on to the next. During a time of practice, toddlers can experience much frustration, but once a new skill has been acquired, they experience a great deal of pleasure, especially because most of them receive great praise and responsiveness from adults around them when they learn things. Moving around opens up new worlds for toddlers. They become more coordinated and better able to balance and gain body strength. The combination of their newfound physical abilities and their growing intelligence can challenge their expectations and impact their emotional and social worlds.

Physical Milestones

- Stages of walking: cruising, tentative wobbly walking, steady walking with arms lowered and shifting weight from foot to foot

- Climbing up a small incline holding on to an adult with one hand

- Walking and carrying a toy or object in one hand

- Hand and eye coordination—small muscle growth

Safe Surfaces

- Toddlers love to move, so they quickly go from walking slowly to picking up speed.

- Their bodies lean forward, making them prone to a lot of falling at first. Try to keep your toddler on safe surfaces when she starts walking.

- When she is inside and walking, try letting her go barefoot. This will help her steady her feet on the floor and acquire better muscle memory.

Parents must rein in their own expectations as their child changes and grows. We have to keep toddlers safe as they move around more freely, as well as set limits. From a toddler perspective, this makes no sense. For weeks we have cheered them on as they learned to walk, and now we tell them, "No. You cannot go there." This conflict is often the first between a parent and child. Part of parenting now is to create space for a toddler to practice in as unrestricted a way as possible. If couches for climbing are going to be off-limits, what else can you use to challenge your toddler? Be creative.

Shoes for Walking

- Because they are eager to try things out, it is important that you buy your toddler shoes that fit well and that have good soles that grip well.

- Shop early in the morning with your toddler when she is rested and more likely to try on shoes. It will take her a few days to get steady in shoes, so she may be more prone to falling at first.

Climbing

- As toddlers venture outdoors, they will also be pulled toward climbing.

- Many toddlers get very excited when they see things they can climb up on.

- They are surefooted going up, but cannot reverse their thinking yet to see how to climb down, so they will need your help.

- They are also not able to assess the safety of the climb, so be watchful and stay close.

EMOTIONAL DEVELOPMENT

Feelings just happen, but what toddlers do about them is part of their emotional development

Emotional development is as much a part of 12- to 18-month toddler development as learning to walk or talk. The challenge is that much of this development is happening internally, so we're not quite sure how to understand what we are seeing in our toddlers. We begin to puzzle out what we think is going on. The extra challenge is that our emotions are weighing in as well. Our anger, sadness, or disappointment as our toddlers start to act out their own experiences can complicate our reactions to them when they express these feelings.

When toddlers begin to express themselves emotionally, parents often find themselves losing control and sounding

Beginning Emotion Coaching

- Listen to audiotapes of John Gottman's books on Emotion Coaching.

- Try to identify emotions your child is expressing.

- Set realistic expectations for your toddler—if you don't want him to touch toys in a toy store, don't let him out of the cart or don't bring him along.

- Toddler reaction can be strong but is usually short-lived at this stage. Young toddlers can be redirected more easily than older toddlers.

- Read simple books to toddlers about emotions.

- Know your emotions so you do not burden your toddler.

Putting Words to Feelings

- Toddlers show a wide range of emotions, some of which are very easy to read and others that are not as understandable.

- When you see your toddler reacting to something with pleasure or joy, give her some feeling words. Say, "I see your smile. It looks like you are happy." This helps her put words and feelings together.

more like their own parents than they ever imagined possible. Toddlers imitate and model what they see and are looking for an emotional glossary to help them understand what it is they are feeling inside. Our job is to give them a map of the landscape. If they are angry and we respond only in anger, they will not easily learn other ways to handle their own anger, except to let it escalate as they see it modeled.

Young toddlers can detect differences in our moods even if they do not understand them. We need to be aware of this as we navigate our own emotional responses in everyday situations. If toddlers are frustrated, we must remember that they are just learning emotional language and have very little experience with feelings. We need to show them we can tolerate their feelings without falling apart ourselves. We cannot pick our feelings, but we can decide what to do about them. This is the most important thing we can teach our toddlers, as it will affect the way they navigate relationships with everyone in their lives.

Angry Feelings

- In the middle of her anger, your toddler may not hear all your words, but it is still important to offer her some language.

- Say, "You are so angry right now. I see how mad your face is." This will help her understand that you get what is going on.

- Toddlers are not cognitively aware of what is happening in the moment they are having such a strong reaction.

Sad Feelings

- Toddlers experience sadness, and it is sometimes harder for us to see them sad or really unhappy than it is for them to experience the feeling.

- When your toddler is sad, she may cry or just withdraw. Continue to offer language that describes feelings. Say, "I think you are feeling sad right now."

- Providing emotional language does not change the feeling, but it is a way for toddlers to begin to process the experience until they have more verbal skills.

SOCIAL DEVELOPMENT

How comfortable a toddler is socially is part temperament and part learned skill

The social development of a 12- to 18–month-old toddler is complicated. Toddlers are eager to get out in the world, and at the same time they want everything to stay the same. They take pleasure both in watching and participating in activities at this stage of toddlerhood. Some weeks a visit to a playgroup goes without a hitch, while other times it is a scene full of tears and frustration. As toddlers are exposed to more social experiences, they are trying to learn the complexity of social interactions. Rules they understand at home do not seem to apply in the same way they do when they are out.

Toddlers are observing behaviors and trying to organize their thinking to match what they are seeing. Their social

Social Developmental Milestones

- Interest in other people

- Some sharing, such as handing dad a Cheerio and then taking it back

- Learning social situations through trial and error

- Playing alongside a peer and imitating play

- Some increased anxiety in new social situations

Social Awareness

- Toddlers begin to make more meaningful connections with grandparents and other adults as they venture out into the world.

- They will be able to remember some of the experiences they had or feelings they felt for the other person and use that information to reconnect.

needs are very simple—they are curious and want to see what and who is out there. Toddlers at this age are still very focused on their own needs. They are experimenting with sharing and unaware that other children have the same needs or feelings they have. When a toddler is developing social skills, he may take another child's toy out of his hand—not because he is selfish, but because he can't really fathom that the other child wants it, too.

Observing Other Children

- Toddlers at this age are very aware of other children. They are noticing what play is like or what another child is holding.

- At this age, toddlers are not aware that other children may feel the same, think the same, or want the same thing that they do.

- It takes time for them to see that other toddlers have the same needs and desires they do. As your toddler begins to realize this, she will start to see herself more connected to other children.

Getting Out

- Toddlers love outings and observing in the world. They will point to dogs, bugs, and more.

- Your toddler may appear fearless from a distance, but as she approaches things, she may hesitate and become more cautious.

- Describe what she is experiencing. Say, "That dog is much bigger now that we are close." Be matter-of-fact and don't convey your own feelings if you are anxious.

- Some toddlers are not comfortable saying hello. Give them some time and practice with stuffed animals.

LANGUAGE DEVELOPMENT
A toddler is ready to talk when she is listening and understanding much of what she is hearing

Toddler language is about learning to communicate and realizing there is shared meaning in words. The development of language happens in an interactive environment. Toddlers' first words are usually nouns, particularly names. As toddlers develop vocabulary, they are also linking mental concepts with a set of sounds. While this is happening, the toddler is also trying to understand tone and intention, which involve both cognitive and social developmental concepts. Toddlers pick up these concepts pretty quickly because they are extremely motivated to have their intentions understood. They will model what they hear.

At first, toddlers use gestures combined with words to

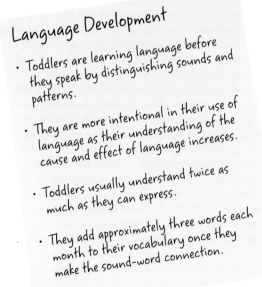

Language Development

- Toddlers are learning language before they speak by distinguishing sounds and patterns.

- They are more intentional in their use of language as their understanding of the cause and effect of language increases.

- Toddlers usually understand twice as much as they can express.

- They add approximately three words each month to their vocabulary once they make the sound-word connection.

Receiving Language

- Toddlers are wired to communicate. They are busy hearing sounds, words, tone, and effect when you speak or sing. They are paying attention to the rise and fall of your voice and the patterns that come with speech.

- Even before your toddler can express words, he is receiving information about how language works, so provide lots of opportunities by reading, talking, and singing to him.

communicate. They will not rely completely on words until they have a larger vocabulary, at 18 to 24 months of age. The ability of a toddler to understand what is said is called *receptive language,* and the ability to speak is called *expressive language.* Toddlers between 12 and 18 months can understand 50 to 70 words and speak about 10 words. By 24 months, expressive language still lags behind receptive language but is catching up. This balance will shift dramatically as toddlers approach their third year.

Toddlers use language to organize their experiences and begin to understand their inner life and share it with others. Early talkers do not have a lot of emotional language because they are still very focused on processing their world in a concrete way. As they become more aware of others, they will begin to show an increased understanding of their world through words.

Making Connections

- Your toddler opens and closes loops of communication with you throughout the day.

- When he says "cookie" and you hand him one and say, "Here it is," you are teaching him that his words have meaning and that you understand that meaning.

- As your toddler experiences this feedback, he makes more brain connections that help move his language forward.

Phone Curiosity

- Toddlers are endlessly fascinated by telephones. They see you using something and see you talking, but they are not able to understand conceptually the meaning of the phone.

- What your toddler does see is that you are not really present with her when you are on the phone. She sees that you are distracted, and that can be difficult for a toddler. Her behavior changes and she can become more demanding as she works to get your attention.

SELF-ESTEEM
Feeling good about yourself starts at birth

Toddlers develop a sense of themselves in relationship to others. Before 18 months, most children do not recognize themselves in a mirror. They are still unclear that what they see is their own image. Their experience of themselves up to this point is dominated by how they see us seeing them. When you look at your child and coo or tell him he is wonderful, he experiences feelings of pleasure and connectedness or attachment to his primary caregiver. Out in the world, he will look to see if he has this effect on others. When he does, it will help give him a sense of security. When he does not, he will look to you for validation and an understanding of why this feels different.

It is our job to help children navigate social situations, but this does not happen easily during the first two years

Developing Self-Esteem

- Self-esteem is a movement toward independence, and toddlers both want to stay close and move away.

- Toddlers start to form their own goals for meeting their needs.

- Awareness of how the world works is becoming more evident, including some understanding of how their parents feel about some things.

- Toddlers look to us to reinforce what they are feeling and doing.

- They need help with understanding limits; try to avoid shaming them while explaining those limits.

Mirroring Back

- When your toddler sees you looking pleased or proud, it communicates love and contributes to a developing sense of competency.

- When you see your child looking pleased when he accomplishes something, point it out.

- Praising can become meaningless after a while, but letting him know that you saw how good he felt when the blocks went into the shapes affirms his sense of himself in a positive way.

of a child's life. The toddler is still egocentric and cannot empathize with another's point of view. It is important that we help toddlers understand limits in a way that does not induce shame or embarrassment. Toddlers need help in separating their behaviors from their sense of self. They are not bad because they hit, but hitting is behavior that is not good because it hurts someone else.

*** GREEN ● LIGHT ***

Say this to a young toddler who has just hit: "It is not okay to hit your friend. I see that you want that toy, and it is hard to share. I will help you while you wait for your turn." This language will still set a clear expectation of behavior for a toddler without causing her to see herself as bad.

Recognition of Self

- Your toddler wil begin to recognize himself in the mirror between 15 and 24 months of age.

- Recognizing his own image is an important part of his developing concept of himself as an individual.

- This is a good time to start making small photo albums for your toddler to look through.

Are You There?

- Your toddler will often check back and look at you as she walks away. She is ready to move farther from you but needs your face as an anchor, especially when you are out of the house together.

- She may need time to warm up before she moves away from you. She will build her self-confidence, slowly at times, but it is steady work when you let her move away at her own pace.

23

SCHEDULES & ROUTINES
Toddlers do better when they can predict what will happen next

In many ways, schedules and routines are the bones of how a toddler makes sense of his world. Because language is just budding and emotions are still unnamed and not understood, a toddler cannot tell his parent that he is tired and needs to slow down, so he counts on us to read his cues. The challenge as a parent is figuring out the first cue, rather than the last one that may lead to a complete meltdown. That is

the beauty of a schedule—it says to a toddler: Here is the plan, so relax. You do not have to work to show me what you need. I have it covered.

Most toddlers respond to schedules with relief. Not every day is smooth, and not all goes as planned, but a schedule allows both parent and toddler to organize their internal and external worlds. Transitioning from one routine to another

Starting Points

- Schedules are easy to make, but toddlers do not follow them at your will. It can take you over an hour to get your toddler dressed.

- Some toddlers will be easier to move along if you remind them of what is next, while some need to play first before they are ready.

- Knowing your toddler's temperament helps you organize routines for her in a less conflicted way.

Morning Schedule

- Wake up, anywhere between 6:30 and 7:30 a.m.

- Breakfast. Wait until your toddler has had some play time (this can be very short).

- Get dressed.

- Possibly a nap. Toddlers outgrow this early nap by 18 months but until then the rule of thumb is every 2 to 3 hours.

- Small snack and book time.

- Go out, rain or shine. Unless there is a tsunami, get out to walk each day.

- Run errands. Try to limit this to an hour.

does not always go smoothly, and this is sometimes a challenge of temperament. Some toddlers may need help with adapting, but adjusting will be easier if the toddler knows what will come next.

Schedules also give parents a way to deal with long days and the need to keep a toddler occupied. It is important to remember that you will not have as much time as you used to for housework, errands, or phone calls. This 12- to 18-month period is full of quick moments and no sustained attention span. But it is also a time when parents can really find pleasure in watching their toddler learn through play and imitation.

Transition Time

- Toddlers like to go, but going is a two-step process. First, the readying or the transition occurs, and then the going. It is the transition that for many toddlers presents more challenges.

- Toddler attention span is short, and when we are pre-paring them for an outing, they are not able to hold all the steps needed in their thinking.

- Try building in extra time whenever you can, and keep the preparation step separate from the going.

Afternoon and Evening Schedule

- Lunchtime. Try letting your toddler help you prepare lunch, to ease the transition.

- Nap.

- Snack.

- Music time. Listen to music and dance.

- Sit on the floor together and play. Try to spend 30 minutes doing this.

- Bath time. An early bath can relax bedtime pressure for both of you.

- Dinnertime.

- Bedtime. Try to start the bedtime routine no later than 6:30 p.m. to maximize your remaining energy and minimize late-day meltdowns.

TODDLERS & SLEEP

Toddlers need sleep, and sometimes the smallest cues let you know they are ready

Toddlers ideally should have 12 to 14 hours of sleep a day. Making their sleep schedule somewhat predictable helps them get closer to that ideal. Some toddlers between 12 and 18 months will take two naps a day, and others will take just one. The hope for most parents is that a toddler will learn to fall asleep on his own. If a toddler has not mastered this skill by a year, it is still important to work toward this goal, even if it is in small steps. Make sure you have a nap and sleep transitional routine.

When toddlers take short naps (less than an hour), they can actually go to sleep at 6:00 or 6:30 p.m. If they nap for a longer period of time, they can be in bed by 7:30 p.m. each

Developing Routines

- A toddler's bedtime routine is very important, and is the one place that predictability can really help. It allows you, when you are the most tired, to operate from a script and say, "First this, then that."

- The routine also helps ready your toddler and signal that the day is almost over.

- Turn off all electronics—TV, music players, phones—at least 15 minutes before you begin your transition; the fewer the distractions, the better.

Bath Time

- Toddlers usually love being in water in the tub. Try to leave plenty of time for this.

- Sometimes it helps to bathe before dinnertime, so you can start the relaxation process and wind down.

- If hair washing is upsetting to your toddler, try to limit it to a few times at most a week. Practice how it feels to have the water roll down her back and arms before you go to her hair.

night. This routine might include your singing a couple songs together while the diaper is changed, reading or looking at two books together, and then breastfeeding or giving the toddler a bottle. Helping toddlers learn to sleep is not only important for them, but also for parents. Sleep deprivation takes a serious toll on our ability to work and affects how we handle the daily stress of life, including parenting.

Pillow Talk

- Bedtime reading can be one of the nicest parts of the sleep routine. It is a time to relax together, look at pictures, or read a story.

- Bedtime is also a good opportunity to talk about the day you just had. Include some of the happy things that happened, but don't shy away from talking about any bumps you had together.

Cuddling

- Snuggling in at night is wonderful if you give yourself time to relax with your toddler. This is not always possible, but take advantage of it when you can.

- Not all toddlers will let you cuddle them, so do small things like hold her hand, or rub her arms or legs.

- If your toddler is wiggling and wants you to stop, do so. This is not a reflection of your relationship but a combination of her tolerance for touch and how tired she is at the end of the day.

KEEPING TODDLERS SAFE

Toddlers are fast and do not have a good sensibility about safety

Twelve- to eighteen-month-olds are learning many things at one time with the major goal of being more independent. Although toddlers on this journey need to learn limits, they are almost singularly focused on trying everything out there. This makes our job hard: How do we teach them about what is dangerous while encouraging them to feel good taking risks? At the beginning of toddlerhood, we need to create

a safe world at home for exploring and allow toddlers an opportunity to try out their new skills without fear of serious accidents. Toddler physical development can move very quickly, and they can master scaling a bookshelf without any prior notice. It is vital to rethink the home environment on a regular basis.

At the same time a toddler is learning to use her big

Seatbelt Struggles

- Toddlers do not like to be contained, so as they assert their independence more and more, they may resist some of your procedures to keep them safe.

- If you are driving and your toddler unhooks his seatbelt, pull over, stay calm, and remind him that you cannot drive until he is in the seat. This is time-consuming to start with, but after a few times he will understand you are serious.

Stroller Negotiations

- Your toddler may get to the point where she will not sit in her stroller. Pick your battles carefully with this.

- If you can manage it, let her walk or push the stroller for

a while. If you need her to get back in, give her a warning and be clear what you expect her to do. Let her know when she can get out again and walk.

muscles, she is also becoming more coordinated. Her ability to unhook a buckle or safety strap may be a delightful challenge for her but a nightmare for you. Take advantage of the wide range of safety materials available today. We cannot protect a toddler from falling off of a piece of equipment, but we can try to make sure she is not injured.

Grocery Cart Safety

- Grocery carts can be fun, but they present a safety challenge in two ways: They have been handled by hundreds of people every day, and if your toddler suddenly stands up, he can fall.

- Try to do some good hand washing after a store visit, and even if you have a trustworthy toddler, stay close while he is in the cart.

Shelf Climbing

- Shelves can be dangerous when toddlers start to climb. The shelves may topple easily if your toddler tries to climb on them.

- Try testing shelves out when your toddler is not around. Even if they seem safe enough, remove heavy objects from top shelves just in case.

- If there is a particular shelf your toddler is drawn to, try to keep interesting things on the bottom for him to explore and hopefully minimize his interest in climbing.

TODDLERS & TEETH
Taking care of your child's teeth is important to start at an early age

When babies are starting to get teeth, we can clean them with a wet washcloth or gauze, and somewhere around a year we can introduce a soft bristle brush to use with just water. Young toddlers love putting things in their mouths, so this is usually a success, but we need to keep an eye on them so they do not push the brush too far back in their mouth. Keep several toothbrushes around so they are handy after meals. When you brush your teeth, try to involve your toddler in his own toothbrushing and encourage him to brush his tongue as well. Give him a small mirror so he can see his teeth, and encourage him to be proud of how clean his teeth look.

Around 12 to 18 months is also a good time to introduce the dentist to your toddler. Set up some extra time before the

Toddler Dental Care

- Encourage your toddler to drink water.

- Try to serve juice in a cup and limit quantities.

- When your toddler will not brush, see if he will rinse and spit.

- Have a different toothbrush for each person in the family and avoid cross-contamination.

- Wash your hands before you help your toddler brush his teeth.

- Start scheduling regular dental checkups.

Toothbrushing

- At first your toddler might enjoy just chewing on the end of the brush, but this is a process.

- You may still need to wipe her teeth to be sure they are getting clean.

- Let her try brushing your teeth and then see if you can brush hers.

- Modeling is an important tool with toothbrushing.

first appointment so your toddler can look around the office and get the lay of the land. Before you go to the appointment, read a book to her about visiting the dentist. Look at the pictures together and help her identify different parts of her mouth, including teeth, tongue, and lips. Pretend the two of you are dentists and brush all the doll or stuffed animal teeth you can find. Also, take a picture of your toddler at the dentist and hang it up on the mirror so you can refer to the picture when you are brushing your teeth together. There is no reason toddlers have to fear going to the dentist. It is easy to make these visits interesting and even fun. Remember, toddlers like to participate.

New Vocabulary

- When your toddler is learning to brush her teeth, talk to her about teeth, nutrition, and smiles. This helps toddlers understand why you want them to brush and why it is important.

- Information does not guarantee cooperation, but it does help toddlers develop problem-solving skills as they learn more about cause and effect.

Tooth Pain

- Many toddlers are still getting teeth. If your toddler is uncomfortable, try giving her a cold washcloth to chew or put one of her plastic toy animals in the freezer. The cold will help soothe her gums.

- When toddlers are teething they can be more prone to biting, so keep alternatives to people nearby.

YOUR TODDLER'S HEALTH

Toddlers need many well visits, so finding a doctor that helps both of you feel comfortable is important

Toddlers between 12 and 18 months continue to go to the doctor approximately every three months. At each well visit your pediatrician will observe the changes your toddler is making in all the major developmental areas. This is a good time to bring a pre-thought-out list of questions for your doctor to give you some feedback. Remember,

doctors are providing information based on developmental norms combined with their own experience. This is a good starting point, but you may have to factor in your particular cultural or personal values and beliefs as well. It is also important that you feel your doctor is a good fit for you and takes your concerns very seriously. If you feel

Caring for Mildly Ill Toddlers

- Offer lots of water, popsicles, and small snacks.

- Have some different toys set aside for occasions like this to combat frustration. Or put some old toys in a package and wrap them. Toddlers love to open things up.

- Spend more time with your toddler on your lap, looking at books or cuddling.

- Most toddlers who are mildly ill can still go out, so take a walk to get some fresh air. It will help everyone.

Preparing for Well Visits

- When toddlers visit the doctor's office every few months, they may have a mix of feelings and reactions.

- This is a good time to purchase a doctor play kit and

do some imaginative play with it. Use your toddler's stuffed animals or dolls to play out what she might expect to happen. After you look in the doll's ears, have it say, "Oh, that wasn't so bad!"

uncomfortable talking to your pediatrician, you should find another one.

When toddlers go the doctor, they have already had vaccinations or a sick visit so are often resistant to the idea. When a toddler is in the doctor's office, she may be more clingy or unwilling to stay on your lap so the doctor can listen to her lungs or check out her ears. It is always good to be prepared with snacks and books or toys and extra diapers. Try to prepare your toddler for these visits ahead of time with books about doctors or a play stethoscope.

Deciding when to go to the doctor can be difficult. Usually doctors will want to talk to you if your toddler has a fever over 100.5 for more than 24 hours, has vomited more than 4 or 5 times over a 24-hour period, has had diarrhea for over 2 days, has had few or no wet diapers, is tugging at his ear, is having trouble breathing, or is inconsolable. Know your physician's guidelines; always check if you are unsure.

Doctor Visits

- Keep an updated form with information from your doctor visits and a list of questions.

- Be aware of when you need to make well visits so you can schedule them at convenient times for your family.

- Bring a special bag of toys for the examining room. Fill it with engaging items like stickers and a small whiteboard and markers.

- If your toddler appears anxious, remind her of how the doll said it wasn't so bad. Talk about what is happening.

Head Injury Warning Signs

Toddlers fall, and most head bangs are mild. After a fall, seek immediate medical attention if your toddler:

- Has lost consciousness

- Is bleeding from the ears or nose

- Is experiencing nonstop bleeding from the head

- Is experiencing confusion, seizures, headaches, muscle weakness, or vomiting

PREPARING FOR A TRIP

Traveling with young children is exhausting, but minimizing the number of possible conflicts can help

Toddlers love to go places but developmentally have no real concept of time, waiting, or destination. You may have spent hours planning a trip, and after 10 minutes your toddler is ready to get out of the car seat. Knowing the stage your toddler is at really helps. It gives you a more realistic expectation of what may come up for you en route or at your destination.

You should also prepare yourself for the possibility that your toddler will behave differently than you expected in new surroundings.

If you have an active toddler, she may want to stand on the seat of the plane, so you will need to come up with some ideas for takeoff and landing, when standing is not an option.

Entertaining on a Trip

- Sing along to music in the car. Clapping hands and shaking feet allows for some movement in a limited space.

- Try unrolling masking tape together. It fascinates young toddlers. Turn it into a ball that sticks on the seat in front of you or on the window.

- Bring a puppet. You do not have to use a funny voice—just talk and engage your toddler in a story.

- Bring little snacks in a variety of containers. A handful of crackers in different-size containers makes an interesting cognitive challenge.

Car Trips

- When you have a long drive, try to locate playgrounds or malls where your child can run around.

- Try to break up the drive every two hours so your toddler can stretch.

- Toddlers will not want to sit in a high chair for very long after getting out of a car seat, so bring food and eat it while you play at a rest stop. After some playtime, your toddler will be more apt to get back in the car seat.

If you are driving, you may have to make extra stops to let your toddler roam around. It is also important to bring familiar things for toddlers so that when you get them ready for naps or bedtime, you can stick to routines that work at home for you. Give your toddler time in his new crib or bed at the hotel or grandparents' house before bedtime.

If you are visiting family, it is also important to prepare them for the stage your toddler is in. Let them know that he does a lot of climbing or reaches up to take things off tables so they have an opportunity to do some toddler-proofing. Not all families will make these changes, but it is considerate to give yours a heads-up and good to know whether you will need to plan more excursions to a park or mall to allow your toddler some roaming room.

Airplane Travel

- Toddlers may need extra help settling in on their plane ride. Once you have done some traveling with your toddler, you will know whether boarding a plane early is helpful or if it is better to wait and let him run around the gate or play with you until the very end of boarding.

- Try not to strap your toddler in until the very last minute so you can hold or comfort him if he is overtired and irritable.

Packing Tips

- Bring a small carry-on that has everything you need for the flight, with items organized in pouches or Ziploc bags to avoid rummaging.

- For long trips, break snacks and toys into categories: early travel and end-of-day travel. This allows you to plan ahead what your toddler may need according to the length of trip.

- Put a snack or extra water bottle in a bag for yourself; pack an emergency kit with Tylenol for both of you.

TODDLERS & FOOD

The relationship toddlers have with food is inconsistent at best and changes minute to minute

Feeding toddlers can be both gratifying and challenging. It is exciting to watch them move toward independence when they pick up a cracker and eat it with their own hands, and worrisome when they toss everything onto the floor or refuse to take a bite. Two important things to remember: Toddlers are just as interested in eating a dirty cracker off the floor as they are in eating an organic meal you took hours to prepare, and meals would be over in minutes if they had their way. So how do we get comfortable with toddler mealtimes? The most important thing is to reset our own expectations about feeding our toddlers. They eat when they are hungry, and stop when they are full. In short, they eat the way most adults should.

Toddler Snack Ideas

- Mixture of crunchy and soft things, such as crackers, raisins, chocolate chip pieces, pretzel pieces.

- Wraps with veggie spread from the deli.

- Pancake rollups filled with favorite fruit. Add a jar of baby-food sweet potato to the pancake batter.

- Tortilla rolled with scrambled eggs and cheese.

- Homemade baked sweet potato chips. Slice potato, spread on oiled baking sheet, drizzle olive oil on top, and bake until crisp.

Toddler Control

- Toddlers may refuse to let you feed them. This can be worrisome to parents if they see their toddler spilling more than she eats.

- Your toddler may be less focused on eating and more focused on asserting independence and mastering mealtime challenges like holding utensils.

- Encourage your toddler to use her fingers. Give her a few minutes to try feeding herself before you offer her food off of a spoon or fork. Model eating your own food.

Toddlers are trying to be independent, so they often want to feed themselves. It's less about what goes in their mouths and more about the experience of holding a spoon. As parents, we worry whether they are getting the right level of nutrition, but we need to be careful that food does not become the center of a power struggle. When we give toddlers time and space, they usually come around. The biggest temptation to avoid is giving toddlers filling but nutritionally void snack foods.

Self-Feeding Struggles

- Allowing a toddler to feed herself is an important part of learning. If this is hard to do, try letting her have one meal a day where she can practice this skill.

- Try putting a plastic mat underneath the highchair to make cleanup easier for you.

- Make sure her serving sizes are small, which is less overwhelming. Try to eliminate negotiating if possible—bartering usually backfires in the end.

Eating Can Be Messy

- Learning to use utensils can take time, and spills happen. Experiment with a few different kinds of feeding utensils to see which ones are a better fit for your toddler.

- Try not to correct, but model the skill. Tell her you are putting your fork into the chicken to pick it up. She will try to imitate until she perfects the technique. Repetition is important for a toddler.

TRANSITIONING TO TABLE FOOD

This is a time when your toddler is exploring food and discovering taste and texture preferences

At around 12 months, if there is no history of allergies and with your pediatrician's go-ahead, your toddler can start eating what you are serving at the table for yourself. Leave a few days in between for allergic reactions to surface. Toddlers like flavorful foods, so don't be afraid to share some of the dishes you enjoy. Continue to offer a few bites at a time, and put the

food directly on the high chair tray. You can begin to put food on a dish when he is closer to 16 months. Until then, you can skip the stage of having the food dumped on the tray and save yourself some dishwashing.

Toddlers love foods that crunch, so offer some thinly cut veggie fries. Or try a muffin with veggies baked in. Don't

Avoiding Power Struggles

- Offer healthy choices to avoid worries about eating too much of one thing.

- Food jags won't last long, so even if your toddler wants only one thing, keep offering her other small choices to try.

- Avoid bribery or negotiation. Your child will not starve, but you may need to offer an extra snack before bed if she has refused food throughout the day. Try to be matter of fact about it.

- If possible, arrange for your toddler to eat with older children. Positive peer pressure can inspire new experiences.

Small Snacks

- Snacking can significantly reduce your toddler's mealtime desire, so try to keep it to a minimum. Ten little fish crackers may be just fine for a toddler, even if she would eat more if offered.

- Offer healthier snacks to your toddler so you have less to worry about if she does not eat much at mealtime.

be tied to a particular kind of food at a particular time of day. Toddlers love pasta in the morning, and often will be more adventurous early in their daily routine. They also prefer grazing or smaller meals to eating three large meals a day.

If your toddler has a small amount of food at breakfast, try offering some cut-up pieces of boiled sweet potato during a stroller ride. Toddlers like to dip, so take along some yogurt for dipping and water for them to drink when you are out and about.

When you get to the park, offer some red beans. Toddlers do not get hung up on the time of day, and by the time you hit lunch, if your toddler just eats a small cup of yogurt or applesauce, he has actually had a pretty good balance of protein and carbohydrates. Toddlers can be very resistant to being fed, so try to curb your instincts to fill them up, and let them manage their food choices.

Time for Small Table

- Some toddlers love to sit at a table that is more their size. Set the mealtime mood by letting your toddler help you wash off the table with a sponge and get ready for lunch.

- If you are going to keep the table out for other activities, put the chairs away so your toddler cannot climb as easily onto the table itself.

High Chair Struggles

- Toddlers start resisting high chairs at some point during their second year. They know that mealtime means staying still, and this is not easy for a toddler.

- Provide your toddler with some ways to help set up her tray. Give her a choice of colored bowls. Let her help serve her pasta to the tray.

IS FOOD SO IMPORTANT?

Food is like many other things to toddlers: They want to try it, master it, and quickly move on

Toddlers are so busy during their second year that it is hard to get them to sit to eat. It is important to know how much and what types of food they really need. Young toddlers need approximately 40 calories per inch of height, or about 1,300 calories daily for the average toddler. These calories should include foods from each of the major food groups, avoiding

trans fats as much as possible. It is also important to provide approximately 16 grams of protein a day. Most parents do not have the time to measure and weigh food throughout the day, so it is a good idea to get in the habit of serving protein-rich snacks.

Toddlers need color variety as well as taste variety in their

Growth Charts

- Growth charts vary for gender and age, so make sure you pick the right one.

- Growth charts can help us see progress in steady, small ways, but remember that toddlers differ in their rate and speed of growth.

- Children between 6 and 18 months of age will normally move up or down on their percentiles.

- Growth chart information is only one predicator of your child's height. Overall health, nutrition, and heredity all play a role.

Food and Sleep

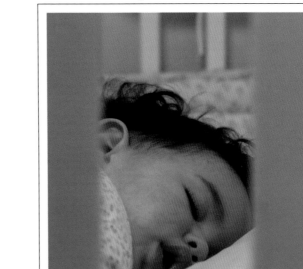

- Toddlers experience night waking for various reasons, but hunger is usually not as much of a factor as we think. Toddlers eat as much as they need, so offering choices that are healthy is a more important goal.

- Focus more on *what* a toddler is putting in her mouth than *how much* she is putting in her body.

foods, so use the rainbow as a guideline. They do not care if you serve the same food for several days. If they like it, they will eat it. If you use approximately their fist size to measure portions, you will be pretty close to providing them with the right amounts. Do your best to avoid coaxing or bribing your toddler to eat. If food is used as a reward, children can develop a negative long-term relationship with it and run the risk of developing eating disorders later in life.

Toddler Grazing

- If your child is a grazer, try to focus on more nutritional foods rather than snacks.

- Cut up dinner leftovers and put them in little cups or bags for her to snack on during the day.

- Mix foods up by color. Serve green spinach pasta one day, then red pasta you cooked in beet juice from a can. Both add nutrients to the preparation.

Drinking Water

- Young toddlers do their thinking and playing in two-hour blocks. They are not able to let you know directly if they are thirsty or hungry. If your toddler has been playing for a while, it is important to offer him water. Also try giving him his own water bottle or cup so he can drink as needed.

- If he is getting irritable, try reading or singing before you offer a snack to see if he just needs a way to transition.

TODDLER EATING HABITS

Part of the eating experience for a toddler is touching and mashing the food

Toddlers prefer eating with their fingers, but you can begin to introduce utensils between 12 and 16 months of age. Small spoons and forks can be very helpful for spearing food. At first, toddlers will observe and model what you are doing with the utensils and then will quickly want to try it out for themselves. They will also experiment with dropping these things on the floor. After the first few times picking it up for your toddler, ask her to use her fingers, and try again the next day. If she continues to drop things, quietly remove whatever it is she is dropping, and say, "It looks like you are finished eating and ready to come down."

If you take your toddler out of her high chair because she is

Sippy Cups

- Toddlers transition from the breast or bottle by way of a sippy cup. During transition, some toddlers refuse milk from anything but their bottle, but this will change.

- There is a wide range of cup choices. Experiment with one at home, and give your toddler a week to see how she is adapting. Two-handled cups usually work best.

- Try to use water as much as possible in the cup because toddlers tend to hold the liquid in their mouths before swallowing.

Toddler Utensils

- Finding the best food utensils for your child can be challenging. Avoid plastics that have PCB in them.

- Toddlers are experimenting with different grips. Have a few different-handled spoons and bowl types to give your toddler practice with different angles as he uses his hands and fingers to develop hand-eye coordination.

- Let him try both forks and spoons. He will show you which is easier for him.

throwing food or utensils, she may want back in right away because she is actually hungry, or because she wants another opportunity to throw things. Try waiting for 15 minutes, and then start over to emphasize that eating and play are separate activities. Your toddler is experimenting, so it may take multiple times over days or weeks to reinforce this important message. Once she understands the distinction, however, pleasant family mealtimes will be possible. Remember, your toddler is beginning to put cause and effect together.

Toddler Dumping

- Young toddlers dump, and this may not be a battle you want to take on. Try putting food directly on the high chair tray. If you do use bowls or plates, only put a small amount of food on them.

- Once a toddler begins to dump, that usually becomes her focus, not eating. Count to 20 to keep yourself cool, take the dishes away, and gently put her down. She will get the message after a few times.

Dining Out

- Eating out with very young toddlers is just not relaxing unless they are asleep. Try to eat out during off-hours, or at places that are really geared to families.

- Limit your own expectations. This is usually not a good time to work out a partner relational problem or catch up on important family matters.

- Try not to go too hungry yourself. You may only get to eat a small amount and have to take the rest home with you.

FAMILY MEALTIME

Family mealtimes should be written on our calendars in ink to help us keep them a priority

Mentioning family mealtimes can bring a range of negative reactions from parents and children alike. But family mealtimes can be wonderful if we set appropriate expectations and start off early with our toddlers. The most important part of these family rituals needs to be the gathering, not the food. The meal itself is really like the icing on the cake.

When you plan family mealtimes, it is important to be realistic about how many times a week you can all sit down together. Once you set a number, honor the dates the way you would any important event on your calendar. If you cancel for last-minute things, the message you will send your children is that this time can be preempted if something

A Time to Engage

- Family mealtimes have the potential for enjoyment, better nutrition habits, more positive attitudes about life, time to plan for the near future, and built-in check-in times for every member of the family.

- Try to keep expectations for family meal age-appropriate. Toddlers may only last for 15 minutes. Try putting some special toys near the table once a toddler needs to get down so you can continue to engage with your older children at the table.

Getting Children Involved

- When you begin to experiment with family mealtime give your toddler and older siblings a way to participate.

- See who wants to help cut up veggies or fruit, and who wants to wash the table or get out the plates.

- The experience of family mealtime is not the food but the community.

deemed more important comes along. The meals should be seen as an essential part of the family's week.

Once children begin to see that the mealtime pattern is sacred to your family rituals, it is important to focus on the pleasure of the time together, especially since with 12- to 18-month-old toddlers meals may not last for long. Create some rituals to go along with your meals: use a tablecloth, put flowers on the table, and come up with a starting event. This could be a song, story, or prayer if that is more in keeping with your own family experiences. Like making a toast when

you first gather with friends, it marks the occasion as special. Then, put out the food. For toddlers, just a few things on their tray is all that is necessary. When your toddler is done, probably well before you are, it is fine to let him down. He will stay close because he will be drawn to the warmth and laughter.

Family Breakfast Time

- Breakfast can sometimes be an easier time for a family meal on a weekend. Talk about it the night before. Let your toddler know you are looking forward to having pancakes together.

- Ask your toddler if she would like to help stir the batter or crack the eggs in the morning. Setting the tone helps a toddler with predictability and routine and helps you follow up on your intentions.

Mealtime Rituals

- Try to create a beginning and end tradition for family mealtime.

- Ritual can add meaning and predictability to the start of a family meal as well as a shared activity.

- A prayer or song or something playful can start off the time together.

- Marking the end of a meal can also help your toddler transition. Tell a story, clap hands, and touch ears and noses—be engaged with each other. This is what will bring you back each time to family meals.

ALLERGIES

Allergies can be serious, but with information and support they become easier to deal with and very manageable

More than 80 percent of children have some type of food or environmental allergy. The major food allergies are dairy, eggs, soybean products, and wheat. Although most children outgrow these allergies within the first five years of life, we need to pay careful attention to how they react to each new food. Many children who are allergic have some tummy distress, which for a young toddler is usually expressed by fussiness or irritability. They may also have itchiness, with or without a rash. The most extreme reaction is difficulty breathing. Call 911 immediately and administer Benadryl or the epi pen according to your doctor's advice.

If your child experiences breathing difficulty, your doctor

Most Allergenic Foods

- Peanuts and other nuts

- Seafood such as shrimp

- Milk, particularly cow's milk

- Eggs

- Soy

- Wheat

Using an EpiPen

- If you are with another person, have her call 911. While she calls, administer the EpiPen.

- Go to your nearest emergency room after you administer the medication.

- Review the procedure on the box regularly, get a how-to from the pharmacist, and practice with a dummy epi pen model, sold at most drugstores. You can have the pharmacist demonstrate how to use it.

will prescribe an EpiPen for emergencies. If you have a family history of allergies, inform your pediatrician. Some doctors like to introduce new foods to such patients in their office. Allergies can seriously limit food options at an age when food is already a challenge. It is important to help even the youngest toddler understand why she must avoid certain foods. Use simple explanations. It is also a good idea to include toddlers in some food preparation. A 15-month-old toddler can pull apart broccoli florets, and sometimes this investment helps toddlers become more adventurous eaters.

Review Labels

Ingredients

Milled Whole Wheat, Milled Cane Sugar, Rice Flour, Dried Cranberries (Cranberries, Sugar, Vegetable Glycerin, Citric Acid, Sunflower Oil), Cornstarch, Vegetable Oil (Canola and/or Safflower and/or Sunflower Oil), Brown Rice Syrup, Honey, Molasses, Freeze Dried Blueberries, Freeze Dried Raspberries, Freeze Dried Strawberries, Salt, Natural Flavor, Barley Malt Syrup.

Made on shared equipment with tree nuts & soy. Made in a facility that processes peanuts.

Dist. & Sold Exclusively By:
[...] 91016

- If you suspect or know your child has food allergies, it is important that you read food labels carefully every time. Make sure you read through the entire ingredient statement, and don't ignore the warning on the labels that says "This product may contain . . ."

- Despite new guidelines issued by the FDA, it is important that you stay diligent as a parent. It is always better to be safe than sorry.

Hidden Ingredients

PARVE

- When you see a product marked *parve,* it should mean the food has no dairy or meat but may have eggs or fish (always check the label anyway).

- Lactose-free does not mean the food is necessarily dairy-free. Find the other words that mean there is a dairy derivative in the food.

- There can be hidden ingredients, so become familiar with the glossary that is most relevant to your toddler's allergy.

IMPORTANCE OF PLAY

Play is the hands-on work that allows toddlers to really hold harder academic concepts later on

Play, especially in the first six years of a child's life, is absolutely essential to his development. A child's brain takes in vast amounts of information all day long. This information has to be sorted out much like your mail. Some information is kept for later, some is thrown out, and some requires immediate action. If we did not sort our mail, it would fill our halls and floors. For toddlers, information overload can lead to meltdowns and fatigue.

Play is the primary way a child's brain organizes information. Without the opportunity to sort things out, the brain gets disorganized, like a closet without hangers and the clothes thrown all over the floor. Young toddlers are observing their

Stages of Play

- **Solitary play**—from about 4 months.

- **Parallel play**—18 to 24 months. Toddler engages in an activity that another child is engaged in at the same time and in the same place.

- **Associative play**—3 to 5 years. Child engages in play that involves others, but each child has different goals.

- **Cooperative play**—5 and up. Two or more children are actively engaged in a play activity developing social and emotional skills together through a common goal that requires social interactions.

Solitary Play

- Toddlers play alone at this age for short periods of time, sometimes minutes.

- Mornings are often a better time for toddlers to engage in solitary play. Set out some baskets to start your toddler off, and let her explore the rest of her things.

- If you need some time to get something done, give your toddler a task. Let her dump and take out the containers in the kitchen while you load the dishwasher. This is toddler play.

world and trying to put a name and meaning to what they see. To accomplish this, 12- to 18-month-old toddlers persist with repetition, which is why they go to the park and attempt to put everything in their mouths over and over again. From their perspective, there is no reason to think that the tenth mouthful of sand will not taste different—better—than the ninth. They have not yet learned to self-regulate and make different decisions.

····················· GREEN ● LIGHT ··············

Say to your toddler the next time she is putting dirt or sand in her mouth, "Come help me fill your bucket. That is not good to eat." Demonstrate the filling and dumping of the sand bucket and then watch how she models what you did. You will have to repeat often at first.

Scaffolding

- Toddlers, when shown how to put materials together, will begin to add this new information to their solitary play.

- If you have shown your toddler how to put his little animals in an empty egg carton, he will remember it the next day and try to do it himself.

- This play is called scaffolding: introducing a new concept to existing play. Use some words to verbalize what you and he are doing.

Watching Is Important

- Toddlers are wonderful observers, so even when your child is reluctant to join play, she is watching, observing, and taking mental notes. Toddlers are gathering information about objects: how to use them and what rules seem to govern play.

- Try not to rush your child to join others until she seems ready. She may prefer to have you sit with her on the floor to help her feel safer in venturing out.

49

SOLITARY PLAY

When toddlers play alone, they are integrating what they have seen in the world around them

Solitary, onlooker, and parallel play are the beginnings of toddler play. At around 12 months, most toddlers engage almost exclusively in solitary play. They taste, touch, watch, and listen to toys or objects and try to understand what they do. They learn through observation that buttons on the remote seem to make things happen, and start to recognize cause and effect. When we see our children imitate or model behavior, we tend to give language feedback such as, "That's right. That's how you brush your hair. You look beautiful," and emotional feedback like, "You are so smart. I love you." All this registers in a toddler's brain. She may not understand why she has elicited such a pleasant response, but she is motivated to

Independent Play

- Toddlers can be very interested in the same thing at the same time at this age but do not actually play together.

- Try to let your toddler play independently until she is ready to engage. If you insist too much, it becomes confusing and frustrating. Sometimes this coaxing can result in more territorial behavior from your toddler—the opposite of what you were seeking.

Grabbing

- Young toddlers tend to reach and grab for toys because they do not have a sense of other's ownership.

- On a playdate try to have multiples of the same toy. From a toddler perspective, red and blue shovels are not the same.

- Between 12 and 18 months distraction may still work, too. Try building a sand pile and smashing it with your hand. Most toddlers are fascinated by action and reaction and will move on if you redirect them by modeling another way to play.

try to repeat it. She sees you looking at her and thinks, "Look at how she's looking at me. I must have done something pretty great. Let me try that again."

As toddlers continue in their play, they also pay close attention to others playing. Dad working at his computer or mom on the phone is not seen by a toddler as a parent who is inaccessible to him. He will crawl to you and want to engage with you because he cannot separate your needs from his. This can lead to struggles, as a toddler is attempting to master his universe and cannot yet distinguish his desires from yours.

The same is true when a toddler watches others. She may be content to see how a peer is using a toy and then be completely surprised that when she wants the toy, the other toddler does not release it. Each of these experiences is being registered. The toddler is asking herself, "What does this mean?" Over time, the frequency of similar experiences will start telling a story to a toddler, and she will be able to predict the ending.

Toddler Gym Classes

- Young toddlers in gym classes can be active or they can be overwhelmed. Much of this depends on both the level of stimulation in the class and your toddler's temperament. Before you sign up for anything, see if you can take a sample class and get a sense of the pace and expectations of the staff.

- You can also try staying for just the first half of a class—this might be enough for your toddler.

Older Siblings

- Toddlers love to play with their older siblings, but brothers and sisters can quickly get tired of playing with their younger siblings.

- If you have an older child, ask her to tell her toddler sibling when she is done playing. Your toddler may still be sad, but this helps her with the transition. You may need to stay and play with her while giving her some help moving on.

IMPORTANCE OF TOYS
For toddlers between 12 and 18 months, less can actually be more

Toys are the bricks and mortar of play, so materials that are flexible allow for the best exploration and experimentation. Pots, pans, spoons, cups, and empty milk cartons are all toys to a toddler. They will taste and touch everything they can reach and then begin to show some preferences for one thing over another. For toddlers between 12 and 18 months, toys hold attention for very brief amounts of time. This can

be very frustrating to parents, who are hoping the right toy might let us take a break.

Young toddlers are not very gender-specific in their preferences. This starts to change at around 18 months, when gender differences are now being explored. At this age, many boys prefer moving toys, and girls prefer toys that can be manipulated. Toddlers are also very focused on cause and

Good Young Toddler Toys

- Balls, big and small
- Push and pull toys
- Sorting and nesting toys
- Small riding toys without pedals
- Empty boxes in different sizes
- Musical toys with a variety of sounds

Pouring and Dumping

- Toddlers love to pour and dump more than just about anything else, so provide lots of opportunities for experimentation.

- Try filling a plastic tub with water or cornmeal, and watch your toddler go. Place the tub on a plastic

mat or a towel for easier clean up.

- Toddlers might want to climb in the tub, so be prepared.

effect, so a ball that you put in a box and she dumps out is now part of a larger sequence that she calls a game, and we call tiring. The most important thing to remember is safety. A toddler will put everything in his mouth, so be sure all toys are free of small pieces and loose parts. If you purchase toys for this age group, it is important to follow age guidelines to ensure safety.

Painting and Coloring

- During nice weather, let your child dip and paint outside.

- Or tape a large sheet of paper over a small table and give him some large, chunky crayons to color with. Try handing him one or two at a time.

- Keep them in a small plastic container, and have your toddler help put them away when she is done. If she puts one crayon in the box and you put in five that is a good beginning.

Wheels for Toddlers

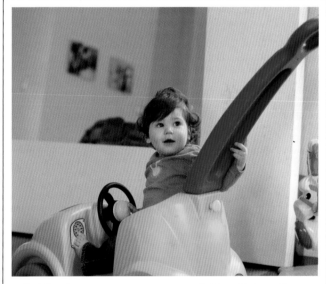

- Toddlers love to move, so look for small, easy-to-mount riding toys. It takes time for them to use their legs, so at first they may prefer to just get on and off the toy.

- Model using your feet to show your toddler how to push himself along. Use words to describe what you are doing so he can begin to make a cognitive connection.

- Practice on soft surfaces at first.

PLAY SPACES

The little space and few things that toddlers need can be organized in a helpful way for them

Play spaces for 12- to 18–month-old toddlers do not have to be large. Toddlers at this age do not need a playroom or a big section of a room filled with toys. Play areas can be set up in part of a kitchen or living room. You can use large floor pillows to define the space and to give toddlers something to crawl on. Small play mats or yoga mats can be used to cover part of the floor to keep the play space defined and a little safer.

Toddlers are usually most eager to play alone in the morning, so make sure that each night whatever toys you have used during the day are back in a box or container, since part of their play will be dumping and spilling them. Choose

Cozy Spaces

- When your toddler is an only child, play spaces can be set up almost anywhere. Toddlers love small areas, so try to define a few spaces in your living room where he can feel cozy.

- Little spaces between furniture are often very appealing to toddlers, so try storing a few containers of toys in these hiding holes to really delight your child.

Sharing Space

- When you have older children, there is always a challenge creating spaces for everyone in the same room, which is usually where they all want to be.

- Use elevated furniture to provide safe havens for older children to play with their building pieces. A folding table would come in handy, or you can gate off a corner of a dining area where older children can spread out.

multipurpose storage containers. A small laundry basket can be used to store balls of different sizes, and when empty to pull around or climb into.

Kitchens are good places to set up a play area. Toddlers love to crawl in and out of cupboards and small spaces. If the cupboard is large enough, you can even put in a small pillow for snuggling (make sure they cannot get locked in). You can also keep some little plastic containers filled with smaller toys to chew on or drag around. Toddler spaces can be changed about once a month with a variety of different objects. It is also handy to keep an iPod dock or radio in a few rooms so you can play music when you are trying to get things done around the house. Toddlers love music.

Make sure the furniture in a play area is secure. Young toddlers are very adept at climbing shelves and entertainment units, so be sure they are securely attached.

Toy Storage

- Keep storage simple. Buy large buckets to facilitate cleanup at the end of the day. Group toys according to use.

- Building materials and cars can go together, as can play people and dishes. If the system is too complicated, toddlers will be more reluctant to help, which means more work for you.

- Toddlers are not able to clean up as they go because their activities are still very connected, so wait until bedtime is approaching before you start.

Toy Safety

- Follow age and stage guidelines on toys. Even an intellectually advanced child may be tempted to place a small object in his mouth. Don't assume your toddler is past that stage.

- Make sure the paint on toys is not lead-based.

- Look for toys that are securely made— toddlers can twist and chew off small parts.

- Uninflated balloons can be choking hazards.

- Purchase a choke tube to be sure small pieces are toddler-safe.

- Check periodically for safety recalls.

GREAT TODDLER BOOKS

Books open new worlds for toddlers, as they match real-time experiences to what they see in stories

Reading books to toddlers not only can benefit future academic success, but also provides closeness and intimacy in the moment. Relaxing together becomes a shared pleasurable experience. This sends a simple but powerful message to a toddler that reading is a way to have loving interactions with his parents. The way a toddler brain works, he will want to come back for more and more. Soon you will be bombarded for requests for "one more book!"

Toddlers are so excited about words that looking at a book together means you get to introduce more and more language to your child in the most natural possible way. Some young toddlers will want to chew on a book or hold it

Active Reading

- Reading to a young toddler can be an interactive activity. If your toddler is not likely to sit still for a whole book, try just showing her a page.

- Ask your toddler to find something in the picture, such as a ball. Ask her to find her ball and bring it over, and talk about the two balls. Little by little your toddler will become more engaged in the book.

Toddlers love . . .

- books with colorful pages

- books with animals and objects they can identify

- few words and easy-to-recognize pictures

- rhymes and alliteration

- books that reflect things in their own lives: moms, dads, dogs, cats themselves, so while they do that, use another book to point out pictures or talk about what you see. After a few minutes, she might grab that one, too, but persevere playfully. Point out colors and shapes, look for the kitty in the picture. This back and forth interaction is a way to encourage more active participation in learning. It is the interaction between the two of you at this time, and being around books together, that will start to hold her attention.

Peeking at Books

- If you keep books accessible, your toddler will be drawn to them, even if it does not happen at first. Keep a few in each room of the house, and change the titles each month (libraries are great for this).

- Use small baskets to store books, or set up a small sitting area where your toddler can relax and look at the pictures.

- The more you read to your toddler, the more he will learn to enjoy books.

Story Times

- Story times are engaging for toddlers, but sitting still for even one book can be difficult. This is not predictive of reading success. If it does not bother you that he is busy getting up and down, keep coming back to the activity.

- Toddler behaviors can be contagious; if one toddler gets up, yours might too.

- Librarians are good at keeping things interesting with songs and puppets as well as stories, but it takes time for toddlers to get acclimated to new settings and expectations.

PLAYING WITH YOUR TODDLER

Playtime is not always easy for adults, but your toddler will be learning with you

Toddlers are learning how to be both emotionally attached and independent. To accomplish this, they need to feel secure and comfortable. When a toddler feels safe emotionally and physically, she can invest more emotional and cognitive energy in figuring out how the world works. Since play is the way a child begins to organize her world, the interaction of another person in play has a significant influence on self-esteem, language development, and communication.

We cannot play all day with our toddlers, but we can identify two 20-minute periods during which we focus our attention and energy on them and nothing else. When we play, or do this "floor time," it means we are going to try to have warm,

Roughhousing

- Men tend to play differently with their children. There is more physical contact and pushing of play to the limits.

- This kind of play is very important to young toddlers. They learn how to take risks and still feel safe.

- Moms sometimes try to replicate rough-and-tumble play, but if dad is already doing it, your toddler may resist doing it with mom as well.

Engaging in Play

- Sometimes it takes time to engage toddlers in play. It is often repetitive, and toddlers do not like taking much direction.

- Try to let your toddler lead in the play. Rather than

showing her how to build a tower with her blocks, build your own. She will watch and model what she sees more quickly than if you instruct the play.

intimate time with our toddlers. This is not a time to teach, but to be a partner in play. When your toddler hands you a toy and you say thank-you and then offer it back, you have helped him with acceptance and security. This can become a touchstone for your toddler to offer you something else and wait for you to have a reaction. He is learning how to interact with other people.

The connection between the two of you during this time is a way to encourage active, imaginative play that helps children see how they fit into the world. Each parent plays differently, and that is a good thing. Your toddler can experience different reactions with each of you. There is also a difference in gender play. A dad's play style can be more rough and tumble. If your toddler has a special way of playing with her other parent, try not to interfere. You might think things are falling apart, but given time, the two of them will figure it out.

This kind of play can impact a toddler's developing sense of self-control and social competency.

Floor Time

(Developed by psychiatrist and pediatrician Stanley Greenspan)

- Floor time is one-on-one play time.

- Floor time starts with a lot of watching from the parent end.

- Floor time is about letting your child lead the play with you following.

- Try this kind of play throughout the day for short periods of time.

- When you tune in to how your child plays, you can gently help him expand his interests.

Gender Differences

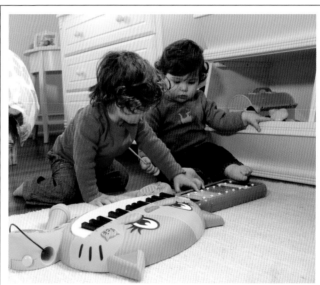

- Boys and girls play differently. Young toddlers are just becoming gender aware, although they make no distinctions between playing near a girl or a boy. Their engagement will be much more interest driven.

- Boys and girls both like to play by themselves. Gender and temperament play a role in how children play, as do cultural expectations.

- Toy preferences may also vary because many boys develop better use of large muscles earlier than girls.

LEARNING TO SOCIALIZE

Social skills are only beginning in toddlerhood; setting expectations appropriately is important

There are many things toddlers need to learn to become effective social humans. Toddlers between 12 and 18 months of age are trying to stay safely attached to their parents and at the same time move out in the world on their own. Every step further from you requires a toddler to master different skills and developmental tasks. She is learning how to share

and reciprocate, how to control impulses, and how to know and follow the rules that exist in the world.

Toddlers have millions of experiences every day with parents, grandparents, and caregivers that are wonderful and model care and giving, and also interactions that are frustrating and confusing. It is the combination of all of these

Learning from Other Toddlers

- Being near other toddlers fascinates toddlers, but they can get into difficulty when their underdeveloped ability to start, stop, and transition is being tested.

- As they are moving from thing to thing, so is their counterpart, and this can cause conflict when they reach for the same objects.

- It is helpful to expect social challenges when you are out with your toddler. He looks to you to guide and keep him safe emotionally in these settings.

Toddler Play Behavior

- Our children are a reflection of us, but toddlers are a reflection of us at their age, not our current age. So it is natural when your toddler does not want to share.

- It can be troubling when a toddler is always grabbing or is always giving up, but this will change with your help. Try to stay as cool as possible. If you can't, it is better to leave a playdate early than blame your toddler for being who he is.

social interactions over time that helps a toddler learn how to regulate her internal experience of herself. It can be a challenge for parents when your toddler is insisting on more autonomy, but we have to go to work or be somewhere on time. So she begins to experience your emotions, and this can confuse her.

A toddler does not have enough language to express confusion, so frustration can ramp up, creating a downward cycle in which we are trying to model impulse control but are almost tapped out ourselves. From a young toddler's perspective, parents are supposed to be responsible for good feelings. Helping a toddler control his own impulses without modeling a loss of your own is difficult, to say the least. Young toddlers are still very egocentric by nature, so factoring in someone else's needs is not on the table. This shifts over time, as toddlers feel more and more successful recovering from disappointment, anger, and sadness. Toddlers need limits to feel successful, so when we can contain our own emotions, they get better and better at regulating their own by watching us.

Special Toddler Relationships

- Not all grandparents can help with child care or give emotional support to you as a parent, but with your help your toddler can learn the difference between family and friend.

- Create memory books together, read stories about grandparents, and call on the phone. All of these repeated experiences help reinforce familial connections and community.

- As you help your toddler feel more connected to his grandparents, you may find they become more connected to him as well.

Siblings Need Time

- Siblings have unique relationships with each other. Over the course of their young lives together, they will experience a range of emotions, including some jealousy or even ambivalence.

- It can be hard for older children to make room for their younger siblings, and younger siblings might feel they have to sneak time with you to avoid upsetting their older brother or sister. It takes time to create emotionally safe environments. Finding regular alone time with each of your children is important.

TODDLER SOCIALIZATION

Toddlers need to experience being with others, but how formally or informally is a parental decision

Young toddlers love to get out in the world. They are naturally curious and eager to see who is out there. Observing is how toddlers learn to socialize. They do not need extensive playdates or classes to learn about socialization. Toddlers in child care or those who are with their parents at home during the day will develop the same skills if we model positive

social interactions and provide them with social and emotional language and help in problem-solving.

Toddlers in a group setting do more parallel play and watching. Some children will get right in the middle of things, and others will hang back to observe and enjoy the play from a distance. It is important when you introduce your toddler to

Group Activities

- Toddlers love to go out with their parents, but not all of them enjoy groups.

- Understanding your toddler's mood, activity level, and body rhythms can help guide you when you consider a group activity.

- Find groups that are not very structured, with room for exploring. Try to minimize experiences that increase your toddler's frustration and your parental disappointment.

Child Care

- There is good toddler day care, but it is up to parents to learn how to evaluate a care setting. Reading or talking to other parents can be helpful, but parents are not all looking for the same thing, so you need to decide which factors are the most important to you.

- Many cities have child-care agencies to help sort out the process of locating care.

- Make sure you visit the facility a few times to observe the program.

a group that there is time for her to warm up and explore with you still safely there. As she gets comfortable, she will venture farther away from you but will still glance back to check on you.

If you decide to join a toddler–parent playgroup, try to talk with the other parents about how to handle conflicts such as pushing, hitting, or even biting. Feeling safe with your peers will help you handle these situations more easily when they come up. Keep the playtime short at first until you see how the toddlers react to each other.

Toddler Excursions

- Some toddlers do better with more open-ended activities, and some will be content in the shopping cart. Try to plan your shopping trips at a time your toddler is rested.

- Let your toddler help hold boxes, or ask him to help you look for the strawberries. Engage him in the activity as much as possible.

Toddler Overstimulation

- Toddlers are beyond overstimulation when they are already melting down.

- If you have been busy and it is going on two hours, your toddler is probably feeling anxious inside.

- If you are feeling overstimulated, your toddler probably is too.

- If your toddler becomes clingy or withdrawn, or pulls you to leave, he is letting you know he has had enough.

SEPARATION: PAINFUL & IMPORTANT

Learning to cope with separation from the people we love is an important part of social competency

Toddlers look to their parents to help them cope with their world, so when it is time to separate, it can be very difficult for your toddler. Sometimes, separations go smoothly; other times, not so much, with a great deal of worry and reaction on the toddler's part. Helping a toddler cope with separation is part of developing social competency. It is difficult to have

our toddlers cling to our legs when we have to leave, and wonderful when they recognize us on our return and jump into our arms. Between 12 months and almost 3 years of age, most toddlers struggle with separation in some capacity.

Separation issues are a toddler's way of saying, "I would always prefer that you stay with me, Mom and Dad." This is

Toddler Good-Byes

- When toddlers begin to learn how to wave, their wave is not connected to the feeling of someone actually leaving. Use words to let a toddler know that someone is going.

- After the separation, remind him that he will see

that person again. This will help when it is your turn to say good-bye.

- Toddlers develop a social, emotional, and cognitive understanding of good-byes with practice.

Tips for Saying Good-Bye

- Tell your toddler where you are going.

- Tell her you will be back, and use her routines to mark time. Say, "After you play and have a snack."

- Tell him what will happen when you go. Explain that Grandma is going to play trains with him.

- Give her something of yours to hold while you are gone.

- Be as matter-of-fact as possible.

understandable, but only because toddlers have no long-range view. When toddlers separate from a parent or parents to go to their grandparents' house or to the babysitter's, they learn about different types of connections they can experience with other trusting adults. Helping toddlers with separating takes time. If we rush it, they will often become more anxious in new situations, so go slow and remember that helping a toddler cope with his feelings safely will be an important part of his social success.

MAKE IT EASY

Here are some tips to help your toddler and you say good-bye: Say good-bye to your toddler, and let her see you go so she does not wonder what happened to you. Help your toddler look ahead by telling her you will see him later. Keep things positive when you say good-bye, even if your heart is breaking. Having your toddler see you look calm will help her reset herself.

Dads Aren't Babysitters

- When you leave your toddler with your partner, it is important to remember that dads are not babysitters.

- Allow your partner an opportunity to problem-solve care when he is alone, and don't leave lists of things to do or plan out the time. It is important that toddlers have the experience of alone time with both of you.

Interviewing Sitters

- Check references and do background checks on all potential sitters.

- Ask your potential sitter what she likes to do with toddlers, rather than telling her what your toddler likes. This will give you a better idea of her skills and development knowledge.

- Give your toddler some time with the sitter before you leave them alone, even if you are going to put him to bed before the sitter gets there, so he will have some familiarity if he wakes up.

PREGNANCY & TODDLERS

You and your toddler are still in the learning stage, so adding another baby will take time

Many families will decide to become pregnant again somewhere during the young toddler years. There is not a good or bad time to introduce a baby into the family based on development, but there may be better times for you as a couple. Some parents will say that it is easier to do all the young baby and toddler work together, while some parents prefer to spread it out. At each stage and age of development you will have to do different things to help your child understand her feelings. Every child reacts in her own way in her own time.

If you are pregnant and you have a very young toddler, the idea of having a baby won't be concrete for him. He will have no idea what this really means. Remember that toddlers are

Introducing the New Baby

- Introduce your toddler slowly to the new baby. Young toddlers do not have the cognitive development to really take in the meaning of this new baby in their world.

- Some toddlers are more fascinated by babies than others. If your toddler seems disinterested, allow her the space and time to get acclimated, even if it takes weeks.

Preparing for the New Sibling

- Let your toddler help create baby spaces.

- Take out baby pictures and talk about what is happening in the pictures. Have your toddler find the baby in family shots.

- Avoid asking if he would like having a sister or a brother—toddlers do not understand the question.

- Occasionally point out parents and babies when you are out. Say, "Look, there is a mom pushing a carriage with her baby."

still very egocentric. They will begin to pay attention to a different tone and energy in the house as the birth of the baby gets closer. Toddlers are good at picking up on excitement or anxiety. Try to keep things as much the same as possible. It can be tempting to try to rush potty training or the move to a big-kid bed, but it is best to follow your child's cues in these areas.

The beginning of your eighth month is a good time to start reading books about babies or playing with a baby doll. This will allow you to introduce some new language to your toddler. It is also important to decide who will watch your toddler when you go into labor. Make sure he knows that Grandma, or whoever, is going to stay with him when you go to the hospital.

Adjusting to a Baby

- If you are expecting your third baby, your toddler will need time to adjust even though she is used to having another sibling already.

- Some toddlers become clingy as you near the end of the pregnancy. Parents cannot split time the same way they did before, so there is often more waiting or taking turns that toddlers will need help learning how to deal with.

New Feelings

- Toddlers are not really sure what is happening when the new baby comes home. They are watching and trying to make sense of the dramatic change in their lives.

- When strong emotion is shown, let your toddler feel her feelings (unless, of course, she is putting the baby at risk). If she says "no baby," mirror back her feelings. Say, "You don't want the baby right now. I can see that." Avoid telling her how much her sibling loves her.

ENCOURAGING FRIENDSHIPS

There is a big difference between forcing friendships and helping toddlers develop friendships with each other

Toddler friendships do not look like our friendships, or at least one hopes not. They are fraught with ignoring, walking away, and regular conflict. Playdates are good ways for parents to share notes but also opportunities for toddlers to see parents model social interactions. When you go on a playdate, your toddler may be clingy or anxious to get to the other child's toys. There is not usually a lot of possessiveness over toys at this age, though you may find toddlers grabbing things they want from each other with no real idea of ownership.

Try to limit playdates so they start and end on a positive note. Usually an hour is a good amount of time to play in someone else's house or your own. You may decide after the

Playdate Tips

- Keep the playdates short.

- Have some toys out that are similar.

- If your toddler is territorial, have more playdates outside your home. This attitude will change, but give it time.

- Create a time to have a snack together and read a book. Toddlers will often sit down together to participate.

- Try to take a rough playdate as nothing more than that—a rough playdate.

- Toddlers may have friend preferences that do not jibe with your needs for matching adult companionship. Try to allow your toddler to have friends that are different.

Visiting Toddler Friends

- Try not to build up a playdate or overcaution your toddler by reminding him that he hit someone last time. If the last visit was rough, this visit has a 50-50 chance of going better.

- Try to manage your own worries. If the child you are visiting is territorial, bring some things of your own just in case.

- Try not to judge—the shoe could someday be on the other foot.

hour that you want to walk together or go outside to a park or playground, which allows your toddlers an opportunity to relax and sit back in their strollers. Breaking bread together, even at 13 or 14 months of age, is a social experience that can be shared. Sitting down to some Cheerios is a good way to introduce a shared activity. It is also a nice opportunity to begin to model some toddler manners. You can ask the toddlers to join you at the table: "Would they like some food?" Use "please" and "thank-you" liberally to set the stage for encouraging children to use good manners as they get older.

As you end the playdate, you can clean up together and wave good-bye as you go. All of these small moments play a large role in introducing social behavior to your toddler.

Teaching Manners

- When you are teaching manners, start with modeling.

- Say "please" and "thank-you" to your toddler so she becomes familiar with the language.

- Toddlers do not make the connection between the word and the meaning yet—that takes more years of practice.

- Your toddler will see you are pleased when she uses proper language, but avoid calling her out in public when she doesn't. Remind her when you are home.

Imitating Behaviors

- Toddlers learn by looking and observing. They often imitate what they see, even if the behavior they saw had negative consequences.

- Toddlers cannot deduce that if they do the same wrong thing, there will be negative consequences for them as well.

- Some toddler behaviors are more contagious than others. If your toddler experiments with the behavior, try saying, "I know you saw Emily push, and her mom said no pushing, too."

SPECIAL OUTINGS

An age-appropriate outing can be joyful for both of you, at least for the most part

Toddlers love new things, so arranging some special outings is a great way to introduce your child to new experiences and share pleasure with her. Trips to a farm or orchard are wonderful, especially if there is also room to roam. Try to plan these trips with no time pressure, so you can come or go as your toddler needs. Bring books along, so if she is getting tired and you need to do a diaper change, you have materials that will engage her. If you are going on a zoo trip, remember that your toddler may not want to stay in the stroller, so pack light. You will need to have your hands free if she wants to get out and walk a bit or be carried. Make sure you have snacks for you both so nobody melts down due to low blood sugar.

Great Wide-Open Places

- Zoos—especially the children's sections
- Aquariums—big, wide viewing spaces
- Farms—fields to run in
- Orchards—trees to touch
- New parks—new equipment
- Hands-on museums—especially the toddler rooms

Toddlers and the Beach

- Going to the beach for most toddlers is a perfect activity. Water and sand, buckets, pouring and dumping—it does not get much better than this.

- Pack lots of water to drink, and use both sunscreen and sun-protected clothing.

- Try to get out in the morning or late afternoon, when the heat is a little less intense.

After a special outing, try to engage in some play that reflects your experience together. Set up your toy animals and build a farm, and talk about what you saw and did on your actual outing. If you took photos, print some out so you can hang them up in the kitchen and talk about them for the next few weeks. Even if they are not yet able to express themselves, toddlers have a tremendous amount of understanding and will enjoy seeing the pictures and remembering with you.

If you take a trip to the beach, make sure you are prepared for the sun. Put sunscreen on your child before you leave and reapply once you get there. Some toddlers will not walk in the sand, and others will not go in the water. Try to encourage your toddler to run around and play, but don't be concerned if he is cautious.

Toddler Classes

- Toddler gym classes can be fun at this stage. Pick a group where your toddler is challenged but comfortable.

- Some weeks go better than others, so try to go with the flow and keep your own expectations appropriate.

- If your toddler becomes more aggressive in group settings, try taking a break for a while. It will get better over time.

Open Spaces

- Toddlers love open space. Malls, fields, and hallways are all toddler play lands.

- If you hit a patch of bad weather, try to find spaces like malls where a moving toddler won't be as much of a problem for others. Stay close and watch them explore.

- Toddlers enjoy the repetition of chase games, hiding and squealing at the same time. This kind of open-ended play is just as important as exposure to a gym or music class.

COGNITIVE DEVELOPMENT
As toddlers walk more, they learn to think more, and vice versa

Toddlers between 18 and 24 months old make a huge leap in memory and intentions. They have a much greater idea of what they want and how to make it happen. They can wake up and be ready to get their boots to go outside, or get a toy you told them they could play with in the morning. They can express themselves more directly with both language and nonverbal communication. At this age a toddler shows great interest in what you do as a parent, including what happens when you sit on the toilet, and often wants to help you with the toilet paper. They do not want to be denied any opportunity to touch and play with materials, and begin to experiment with objects to meet a self-identified goal.

Your toddler may build a tower with her blocks, and then look to you to see if you approve because she now has an

Toddler Cognitive Development

- Intense interest in the world
- Developing conscious expectations
- Awareness when things do not go as expected
- Increased imitation and modeling
- Pre-planning

Hand-Eye Coordination

- Toddlers love to put things in and take things out. Try to provide your toddler with an assortment of toys that can challenge her hand-eye coordination.

- Save the lids of orange juice cans and your empty wipe boxes, and you have a homemade toy that offers days of fun as your toddler spills the lids out of the box and hears the noise they make as they roll across the floor.

internal sense of her accomplishments and self. Not only can she hold a specific intention, she can also remember a sequence with ease. She can get a book, hand it to you, and point out something she found on a page yesterday. Because she is developing more ability to think ahead, this also means she has a sense of what to expect and does not like deviating from the norm.

Toddlers at this age are looking for consistencies to measure the standard of day-to-day living, as that is their world. When their world changes, they have to try to make sense of the change. Toddlers also begin to think about parent reactions and see them as linked to awareness of a feeling inside that seems to increase or decrease with parental approval or disapproval. For toddlers, a lightbulb moment occurs when they hear your words as a thought in their head.

Playing with Blocks

- Blocks are an essential toy for children between the ages of one and six. The size or the material of the block may change, but the challenge to build and create will stay the same.

- Blocks are important for both boys and girls. Boys often build taller structures, while girls build long structures.

- Children learn balancing skills, early math skills, and patterning, which is the basis of reading, from playing with blocks.

Playing with Puzzles

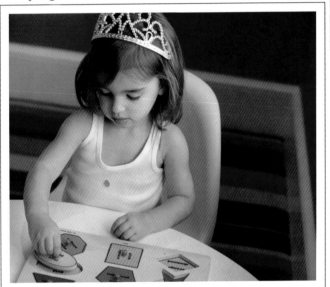

- Puzzles help toddlers with object recognition and space relationships. Knob puzzles are the easiest for toddlers to handle.

- Since puzzles can be expensive, try rotating them with friends. This way interest stays high and skills continue to increase.

- Toddlers may also use puzzle pieces for other types of play. Just gather them back at the end of the day.

PHYSICAL DEVELOPMENT
More and more movement has purpose

Physical development is now being integrated with cognitive development in a much more meaningful way for 18- to 24-month-old toddlers. Once a toddler begins to move around more comfortably, he begins to have clear purpose to his movement. He now uses his walking to get something or to do something. This integration of developmental milestones is a powerful time for toddlers. They can feel their bodies and hear their minds. For us as parents it is also a powerful time because toddlers often increase their persistence to match their internal feelings of wanting to control their universe. This can be exhausting because now when you go to the park, your toddler may want to push the swing himself

Physical Development

At 18 to 24 months toddlers:

- get steadier on their feet;

- start to show more bodily self-control once they begin to walk;

- use their standing skills to propel physical movements such as climbing;

- are able to put together a series of physical skills to achieve a goal such as climbing the stairs to reach the top and then turning around to come back down.

Falling Down

- Toddlers love to run, but they can still trip and fall easily. Try to give your toddler a number of different surfaces to practice on.

- Grass and sand can sometimes bother children who are more sensitive to touch. If this is the case with your toddler, try not to insist.

- Some toddlers are more sensitive to sensory experiences. It can take time for them to feel comfortable and surefooted on uneven surfaces.

or try to climb up on larger play structures.

Toddlers do not yet see that they cannot do everything themselves, which makes helping them even more difficult. One minute you are encouraging them to explore, and the next minute you are trying to keep them from falling off of something dangerously high or unstable. Toddlers are also developing small muscle control, so they have increasingly better hand-eye coordination. They can use a shovel to do a little digging or push a toy around the room without crashing into furniture. They can also hold objects when they are playing and use them in appropriate and meaningful ways.

There are new possibilities for outdoor play with your toddler. Balls can now be thrown or kicked with more purpose and skill than before, and she will enjoy running and jumping with newfound confidence. Indoor play can become more creative, and maybe more hazardous.

Reversing the Climb

- Toddlers climb on almost everything and land in precarious places. If your toddler has gotten up too high on a climbing structure, ask her how she thinks she can get down.

- Help her problem-solve the steps she will need to take to reverse the climb up. This will help her develop stronger cognitive skills and increases her physical agility and understanding of directional language.

Falling Safety

- Toddlers fall, so try to check out the new environments you are bringing your child into.

- Since things happen fast, it is a good idea to carry some Band-Aids and saline solution to clean off a bad scrape.

- Some toddlers are more bothered by blood than others. If your toddler seems upset, use a dark washcloth to clean off the blood and say, "Your body is working just right. It will feel better in a few minutes."

EMOTIONAL AWARENESS

Toddlers will become more aware of their feelings without yet having emotional language

At 18 to 24 months, toddlers are becoming aware that they are experiencing feelings in their bodies that they may or may not find comfortable. They are trying to regulate or manage these feelings. Toddlers will feel happy and begin to connect their happiness to an experience. They might fall and look to you for comfort, internalizing the way they feel as you comfort them. Your toddler's emotions are now also influenced by their feelings of power from moving and thinking. Desires and wishes are increasingly gratifying to them, but sometimes feelings get too big, causing worry and anxiety.

Toddlers assert themselves much more at this age, and experience anger or sadness when they cannot have it all.

Emotion Coaching

- Name the feeling you are seeing your toddler express. Describe how that feeling is experienced in her body.

- Say, "When you were angry you threw toys. I can help you. Would you like this instead? Can I hold you?"

- Talk about how she felt when the worst is over. Say, "You wanted that toy and got so mad you threw it. I am sorry you were so angry, but it is not okay to throw toys."

- When you do not have the energy to emotion coach, try your best not to shame your toddler.

Expressing Emotions

- Toddlers express their emotions with their whole bodies. Joy and excitement are expressed with their arms, legs, and facial expressions.

- Happy feelings are just as important to name as sad ones. Tell your toddler that excitement or joy is a nice feeling, and point out other times she may have felt that way.

- When she is feeling sad at another point in time, remind her that she will feel happy again like when she splashed in the puddle.

The words "This is your last cookie for now" make no sense from a toddler's emotional perspective, and the disappointment must be managed. Their purposeful reactions begin to impact our own emotional world more forcefully. We can shift from being a proud parent of an expressive toddler to a frustrated parent who feels out of control in an instant. The challenge is to help your toddler learn how to control his own impulses. He needs you to coach him emotionally through his feelings, but this can feel insurmountable.

GREEN ● LIGHT

Say to a toddler who has heard you tell him no, "I think the feeling you are having is anger. It makes you angry when I tell you that you cannot have that cookie. You can have a cookie tomorrow. Let's find something we can do together that will help you feel better." It can be tempting to give in, but toddlers will learn to self-regulate with your consistency.

Helping with Anger

- Anger can feel very uncomfortable to toddlers. They experience it as we do—body tension, with headaches or irritability—but do not have the words yet to express it, so they melt down or throw themselves around.

- Your toddler's anger can sometimes trigger your own, so pay attention to your feelings so you can avoid a further explosion. Old anger in us and new anger at our children can quickly turn to rage. Back off, and cool down as best you can.

Helping with Sadness

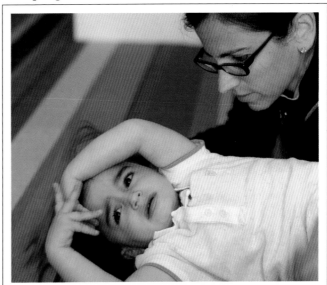

- Toddlers can feel sad not just when they are separating from you, but when they are sick or uncomfortable.

- Since emotional language is still developing, it is hard for them to express their feelings with words, and they are not always able to identify why they are feeling the way they are.

- It can sometimes help to say, "I think when Dad left for work you felt sad. You and he were having a good time."

77

SOCIAL MILESTONES

Toddlers are bringing language and logical thinking more and more into their social world

Toddlers between 18 and 24 months old are generally quite social. Remember, though, that your toddler's temperament will affect his sociability. Toddlers at this stage of development can now remember going to Tommy's house to play, so can anticipate and react to an upcoming event with excitement. Because of their increased cognitive development, they have internalized some of the differences between being at home and going out, so have a better, more comfortable way of accepting the "rules" of behavior. A toddler at home may dump and spill but will be more careful and aware of expectations in someone else's home. They are paying more attention to their surroundings.

Social Milestones

At 18 to 24 months toddlers

- are beginning to see that others have a point of view;

- are starting to get social cause and effect;

- are understanding simple games;

- are beginning to internalize some social rules.

Meeting New Adults

- If your toddler is meeting a new adult, try to make a simple introduction. Many toddlers look away until they are more comfortable with direct interactions.

- If your child appears very shy, give her time. Practice greetings with stuffed animals. Line up the animals and take turns saying hello. Say, "I know, Mr. Bear, that you do not know me. It takes me a little time to look at you and say hello."

Toddlers are still very egocentric, and can only slow down their impulsive feelings so much. They will play closer to peers and pay more attention to other children's play experiences, but proximity may mean more clashes of desire between two toddlers. They may experience more or new symptoms of separation anxiety because they know and can remember what it is like to be away from you. Some may insist on being carried.

At the same time, toddlers' receptive language is expanding. They are successfully expressing themselves through words, which will further their desire to be social.

MAKE IT EASY

When your toddler is clinging, try reminding yourself that this is not regressive behavior but a clear sign that toddler development is like everything else in nature: changing, ebbing, waxing and waning, and moving in mysterious ways. As much as you can, go with the flow.

Importance of Gestures

- Toddlers often use nonverbal language to communicate information. Some toddlers are better able to sense physical space between themselves and other children.

- If your toddler has difficulty gauging appropriate space, give her some cues in play with a stuffed toy. Say, "Hey, Mr. Giraffe, step back. You are too close to my body." These pretend play practices will help her master social cues.

The World Reacts

- Toddlers realize pretty quickly that they get many responses from a wave. This feedback of opening and closing communication circles can feel very good and helps them see themselves as part of a larger social system.

- Your toddler will begin to also see that sometimes he does not get a response, and he will begin to observe different patterns of reaction to him.

LANGUAGE GROWS QUICKLY

Toddlers catch on pretty quickly that words are important in communicating needs and desires

Between the ages of 18 and 24 months, toddlers are excited about their emerging ability to communicate, in part because they see your enthusiasm and pleasure. They begin to realize the power of language and shared meaning that motivates and pushes their learning. You can see more clearly now how your relationship with your toddler and her relationship with you are now more integrated. When toddlers struggle with language development, it is more difficult for them to slow their impulses. They do not have a feedback loop that successful communication provides.

Because toddlers are learning language, they do not always have the right words for concrete objects or abstract feelings.

Language Milestones

At 18 to 24 months toddlers

- have some simple grammar and may put together two-word sentences—"no" may now be "no milk";

- understand the difference between nouns and verbs and that sentences have one of each;

- may know 200 words or more;

- continue to have somewhat creative language and are unclear about the use of certain words.

Toddlers and Music

- Toddlers usually find music very playful. They will begin to predict what comes next in a song, especially if you use hand or body gestures.

- If you aren't familiar with much children's music, try substituting toddler words to a tune you know. There are a number of board books featuring lyrics that you can read to learn the words.

When it is vital they communicate something to you, they may resort to more basic ways of communicating: screaming, whining, or crying. These are ongoing challenges for us as parents. When our toddler can't find words and our frustrations are high, we can resort to less-than-useful tools such as grabbing or yelling, hoping somehow our toddlers will get the message. Sometimes they do, but the process of getting there will not have helped them to understand what to do next time language is not coming easily. Don't forget that you are modeling coping techniques for your toddler.

Conversational Interaction

- Toddlers realize very early in their development that gesturing and language are important because they see how we use communication to meet their needs.

- They watch us talk to others and observe a back-and-forth pattern that helps them understand the interaction of communicating and turn-taking. All of this becomes the groundwork for social development.

MAKE IT EASY

Try pointing out not only what your toddler sees around you, like a dog or cat, but also what is happening to other people. Speculate as to how they might be feeling. Say, "There is another baby crying. I wonder if she is happy or sad? Remember when you cried yesterday because you wanted to walk and not ride in your stroller?" Toddlers will later use the information to help themselves.

Prop Boxes

Set up a special prop box to bring out when your toddler becomes demanding when you are on the phone.

Creating a prop box can be fun. Include things that are intriguing and will pique your toddler's curiosity and give you a few minutes to make an appointment. Try:

- old cell phones
- regular phones
- remotes to old equipment
- buzzing hand massagers

81

FURTHER DEVELOPING SELF-ESTEEM

Toddlers are seeing the impact they have on the world, and that gives them a sense of themselves

Toddler self-esteem is continuing to emerge between 18 and 24 months. We can see more clearly when our toddlers are pleased by their success and dismayed at having made us unhappy. This ability to see themselves through our eyes, as well as their own, is part of the recipe of self-esteem. Toddlers are learning that there is pleasure in pleasing you but also that eliciting that pleasure may be in conflict at times with pleasing themselves. How we handle these conflicts as parents is important because we need toddlers to learn what they can and cannot do, but we also want them to feel good about themselves both ways. There are a few key ingredients in helping toddlers with this task.

Self-Esteem Milestones

At 18 to 24 months toddlers

- can recognize themselves in photos and in the mirror;

- know many, if not all, their body parts;

- are beginning to be sure what gender they are;

- are beginning to remember how things felt and can talk to you about it in simple terms, such as, "I was crying";

- can do some simple problem-solving.

Developing Pride

- Toddlers are learning through their day-to-day interactions how to make sense of the world. They are curious and test their understandings through action.

- How you respond to your toddler is how she learns to respond to herself. When she is stuck and you guide her through problem-solving, she begins to see she has resources within herself to cope with challenges.

Spending pleasurable leisure time with your toddler every day is essential. This can occur at any time, and if all you can make room for is 30 minutes, that is good enough. Remember that sometimes time is like chocolate: A little is better than none. Affection is critical, both physical hugs and kisses as well as verbal expressions of love. You must acknowledge when your toddler has done something well, and you must remember to speak to the behavior—not the child—when he does something that displeases you.

Differences and Similarities

- Toddlers begin to notice more similarities and differences between themselves and others as they move through their development.

- When you are looking in the mirror with your toddler, use descriptive language. Say, "My legs are long; yours are short. I have black hair, and you have brown hair." You are helping her connect her social, emotional, and intellectual development through language and experience.

Need for Closeness

- Toddlers continue to use their parents as touchstones. You are the anchor that keeps your toddler from becoming disoriented as she observes more and more of her world. She looks to you for explanations and guidelines to process all the information she is taking in.

- Some toddlers need to stay physically closer to feel safe enough to do this processing work, while others will orbit a wider circle of space around you.

SUPPORTING INDEPENDENCE
Schedules and routines help toddlers feel more confident about separating

As toddlers get older, they react more positively to routines that are predictable. Since they can now think ahead, they can prepare themselves for what is next, whether it is bath, bed, or an outing. You can begin to ask them to find their shoes or get their coat so you can leave for the park. Their combined skills in the areas of language, thinking, and physical confidence allow them to pull off transitions with more self-control and ease. Of course, knowing what is next does not eliminate all transition challenges because toddlers do not really get this whole "start and stop" thing.

Toddlers may still want to stay out in the living room to play rather than go take a bath, but they will also know what the

Getting Dressed

- Toddlers often begin to assert their independence through resistance.

- If your toddler has a hard time letting you dress her, you can let her pick out a shirt or pants she might like. Offer only two choices so she can make a decision.

- Try to engage her in a story about what you will see when you drive to school or go for a walk. This helps her see what is coming next, and maybe stay still enough to put her pants on.

Leaving the House

- As much as they like to go, toddlers will sometimes not want to leave the comfort of their own surroundings.

- Give your toddler a heads up. Let her know that when you put on your shoes, it will be time to leave. When you start to do this, let her know again that you are almost ready to help her leave.

- Have your toddler say good-bye to what she is playing with, and if you can, let her take something small to hold to ease the transition.

plan is, making it easier if you stick with the schedule. Schedules also benefit parents, who can eliminate the guesswork of trying to decide if a toddler is ready to eat or go down for a nap. This makes for fewer decisions and negotiations throughout the day and for a much more confidant parenting approach.

Having schedules also means that you and your toddler have a baseline, so when you choose to deviate, you can help him adapt to the change but also help him recover after a short-term shift. Vacations are a really good example of this.

When we travel, we can't and often do not want to be on the same old schedule. Your toddler will need help with some adaptations but will try to go with the flow. When you return, you will see your toddler relax more after things go back to what he can predict. Both experiences are important because they help us learn how good change can be for us all.

Offering Choices

- Give your toddler choices two at a time. Children need practice making decisions, and starting early builds confidence and healthy self-esteem.

- When a toddler is making a choice between a banana and an apple, she is exercising the front part of her brain that problem-solves and thinks, and that is going to help her with academic skills later on.

Bedtime Frustration

- Toddlers will challenge bedtime routines from time to time. It is hard for us to stop what we are doing and relax, and toddlers need the practice from an early age.

- We are sometimes so ready for our toddlers to go to sleep that we approach this time with anxiousness or impatience. The message to your toddler will then be one of frustration, not relaxation. Try remembering that the payoff down the road for you will be your child's overall mental and physical health.

CHANGING SLEEP ROUTINES
Nothing stays the same, including toddler sleep needs and challenges

Eighteen- to twenty-four-month-olds may have shifts in their sleep schedule. A toddler who has transitioned beautifully to a bed may not want to say good night to you because he is not happy about separating from you. Toddlers can now also call out to you with words, which can absolutely pierce your heart when you are trying to let them cry it out. They can and

do pledge their love and affection, needing a little more, until you feel like you might explode. The good news is that these challenges are short-lived if you hold steady to your routines and expectations. The bad news is that you may be sleep-deprived for a while.

If your toddler has not been sleeping through the night

Bath-Time Woes

- Even the most water-loving toddler can sometimes resist a bath. It can be related to an increased awareness of their surroundings and what will happen next—bedtime—or he may be remembering soap in his eyes or a bump he experienced yesterday.

- If your toddler shows some of this worry, go slow. Ask him to help you get the bath ready; try using some bubbles or soap crayons. Let him hold the washcloth, and give him a little more control of the process.

Nighttime Challenges

- Challenges can sometimes occur during the nighttime routine. Resistant toddlers can make it almost impossible to get a fresh diaper on or put their legs in the pajamas.

- Talk about what is coming next. Ask, "Do you want the book about the cow or the turkey who lost his feathers tonight?" Sometimes a special song on the iPod can be associated with this part of the ritual. It will help your toddler relax and prepare by looking ahead to what is coming.

before 18 months of age, you may be ready to set up a sleep plan. Older toddlers drop one nap from their schedule. They can usually make it through the morning but need a nap in the early afternoon. Naps are not always long for toddlers, but if they only sleep for 30 minutes, try to leave them in their cribs for another 10 minutes, building up to an hour of rest, even if it is not actual sleeping. Toddlers will sometimes protest a little, but many love the coziness of their cribs and will be willing to wait it out.

Helping a toddler learn to sleep through the night can be challenging, but with time they learn how to do it. If you are ready to set up a plan, commit to not going in every time your toddler wakes up. You may go in to tell her you are there or hold her for a few minutes, but keep encouraging her to do the work.

Lights Out

- Toddlers need different amounts of time to settle in for the night.

- Pick books together, and stick to the number you have chosen. It can help to have one beloved book at the end of your routine as a signal that when that story is over, it will be time to say good night.

- After stories, spend a moment with the light off reviewing the day. Try ending with some cozy words, like "Today was rainy. Tomorrow we will have some fun in the sun."

Slowing Down

- Toddlers need time at night to decompress with you. Some toddlers need more touching, others just your presence for a few minutes before you go. This parting can be difficult because your toddler may have a hard time letting go.

- If this is difficult for your child, tell him you will be back after you use the bathroom to check on him. Remind him to do his job of resting quietly, and be sure to check back in 10 minutes.

AN EXCITING & DANGEROUS WORLD

It is unsettling at times to think about what we need to do to keep our toddlers safe

Making the world safe for a toddler is almost a contradiction in terms because a toddler often sees her job as finding every way she can to test the limits. Eighteen- to 24-month-old toddlers will increasingly resist your buckling them into strollers and car seats with more persistence, and demand more freedom from hand-holding or limit-setting. They see themselves much the way you would imagine a superhero does—fearless and invincible. The truth is that toddlers are caught between their desire to be independent and a growing awareness that they cannot do everything on their own. They now need more language to help understand why they need to stay in their car seat. They want to know why it is important.

Teaching Car Safety

- Toddlers periodically need to be reminded of car safety. If your toddler is struggling staying in his car seat, use this time to play some games like I Spy.

- If there still is resistance, get a puppet that checks on how safe everyone is. Have the puppet be a little silly, checking locks, gas in the car, keys, windshield wipers, and seatbelts. Toddlers at this age are beginning to be drawn to imaginative play and will want to join in with you.

Feeling Helpful while Shopping

- Toddlers need tasks when they are starting to climb out of shopping carts and are resisting being buckled in safely.

- Create a special shopping bag for your toddler with creative materials: an old pocket calculator, some books about going to the store, and an alligator puppet that likes to eat the food at the market. Keep this handy so when your toddler has reached his limit, you have a plan for getting through this time without too much additional conflict.

Toddlers use their burgeoning language skills to organize their experiences in meaningful ways for use in the future. It is important when you are trying to keep your toddler safe to prevent her from becoming overly cautious or fearful. You want her to feel emotionally safe enough to try out new things and stretch in all kinds of ways to learn about her world. Toddlers need to fall sometimes to learn they have to try again. Our job is to help them so the risks do not outweigh the benefits.

MAKE IT EASY

When you go to places that toddlers do not normally visit, check and recheck potential dangers. It is tiring but important to be vigilant. Toddlers make decisions on limited experience and understanding, so we have to fill in the blanks. If you go someplace that may not be safe, plan at least 30 minutes of activities for your toddler in the hope you get 10.

Safety Products

Safety-Proofing Reminders

- Keep your water heater at 120 degrees.

- Test water before you let your toddler get in the tub.

- Lock up matches and lighters.

- Test your smoke alarms once a month.

- Lock up all medicines and vitamins in a cabinet with a child safety lock.

- Know how to call poison control— 1-800-222-1222 or a local number.

- Use safety gates and window guards.

- Use outlet covers.

- Many different companies manufacture safety products. The most important aspects of any of these purchases are ease of use and the commitment to keep it up.

- Covers that are hard to remove may keep toddlers from touching outlets, but parents are less likely to reinsert them once they pry them out themselves to use the outlets.

- Crawl around on the floor once in a while to see what looks unsafe from a lower vantage point.

VISITING THE DENTIST
It may be time to wean your toddler off his bottle or pacifier

About 18 months of age is a good time for your toddler to visit the dentist. He may make suggestions for toothbrushing or eliminating a pacifier or bottle. This does not mean that you have to toss the pacifier into the garbage that second, but it does mean that both your toddler and you will have to prepare for the loss of those very comforting tools—you first. Try to imagine what it will be like to not grab a bottle when

your toddler is fussy so you can begin to think about what you might do instead.

When you're ready, introduce the concept to your toddler. Give him time, and repeat the information every few days so he becomes familiar with the language. Also remember that he cannot imagine a world without a pacifier because his brain cannot do reductive or deductive reasoning. He is

Dentist Tips

- Pick a dentist who is child and family friendly and is responsive to you.

- Have your toddler meet the hygienist before her first visit for a teeth cleaning.

- Practice being a dentist at home, looking at your toddler's mouth, saying "Open, please." Let her practice on you, too.

- Take a picture of your child at the dentist so you can talk about it later.

Working with Your Dentist

- Your dentist can help you learn how to teach your toddler the best way to brush her teeth.

- Ask your dentist about what to expect as your toddler grows and develops, and see if he has any specific recommendations.

- Have a list of questions to ask when you are there, or leave the list with the hygienist if your toddler is upset and you need to make a fast break.

a concrete thinker and will need a concrete plan. When you begin the process of eliminating the bottle or pacifier, decide whether you are going to go cold turkey or move a little more slowly. There is no right or wrong way, and some of this depends on how well you think your toddler will adjust. You can always speed up or slow down as you move through the process.

MAKE IT EASY

When it is time to say good-bye to a pacifier, find a special box to put it in so your toddler can peek at it if he needs to. Remember that out of sight is not out of mind, and often a toddler needs to know the pacifier is still there so he can relax. If he asks for the pacifier, name the feeling. Say, "You are missing the pacifier now. It helps you relax. Can we rock or read a book together instead?"

Toothbrushing

Toddler Dental Care Tips

- Set a fun timer to two minutes to encourage longer toothbrushing.

- Sing a song to your toddler while he brushes.

- Brush before bedtime to lessen the effect of mouth bacteria.

- Try brushing in a small circular motion, cleaning a tooth at a time if at all possible.

- Start in the back and work your way to the front.

- Brush your toddler's tongue if he will let you.

- Have your toddler floss his teeth as often as possible, using a back-and-forth motion.

- Toddlers do better brushing when they can look at themselves in the mirror.

- Set up a dental station with all the supplies. Colorful toothbrushes, fun mirrors, and special floss and toothpaste will make this a positive time.

- Find a fun song to play while brushing.

- If your toddler prefers to brush her own teeth, model some techniques while you brush yours. When she is done brushing, point out how well she did taking care of her teeth.

DOCTOR VISITS
As your toddler becomes more aware of what happens at the doctor, checkups can become more challenging

Children get sick, and sometimes in the middle of their toddler years they get sick more frequently. They are exposed to so much more and still explore a lot of their world by tasting and trying. Sometimes it helps to remember that toddlers are wearing their body fluids inside and out. So when your toddler picks up something from a store, he is both acquiring

and spreading germs. There is no stopping it, so the best we can usually do is try to instill some good general hygiene habits. Hand washing is probably one of the best ways to help toddlers fight germs, and the good news is that most toddlers love water. When you have returned from an outing, pull a stool up to the sink and let your toddler suds away.

Caring for a Mildly Sick Child

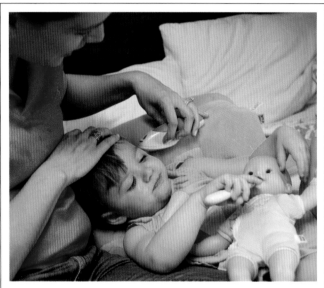

- Toddlers do not lay still for long, so be prepared for them to be up and around.

- Save DVDs for later in the day when you are exhausted.

- Let your toddler play in a sink of bubbly warm water.

- This helps keep her hands out of her mouth or nose if she has a bad cold.

- If your toddler throws up, use comforting words like, "Your tummy is hurting, so your body is telling you it does not feel well. It will feel better soon."

Visiting the Doctor

- Toddlers will probably be less receptive to the doctor when they are sick than when they are healthy.

- Let her stay in your lap, or sit on the exam table with her. Talk to her on the way to the doctor to let her know that he will check her ears to see if they are sore.

- Ask her if she wants to check a doll or stuffed animal's ears. If she does , ask her how the baby is and say, "It was not too bad for her. She is fine now."

When she is done, remark on how clean her hands look and smell. Children will file away this information for later times, such as during potty training.

When toddlers get sick, they usually need a lot of emotional comfort. They are unable to blow their noses, a pretty complicated skill because it requires a series of actions with a specific consequence. They do not know why their head hurts, or why their tummy feels sick, so they are usually pretty clingy or fussy. Asking your doctor under what circumstances she would like to see your toddler is the best rule of thumb when in doubt.

MAKE IT EASY

Make sure you feel comfortable with your doctor. You do not want your fear of feeling stupid to get in the way of reaching out and asking questions. Listening to parents is part of being a pediatrician—it goes with the territory.

Safety and Prevention

- Toddlers can fall anywhere, but bathrooms contain additional dangers. Make sure that the toilet seat is down so your toddler can't fall in head first.

- Use mats on the floor of the tub to prevent slipping.

- Use a cover on the tub faucet to help prevent serious head injury from falling and hitting the faucet.

- Make sure bathroom outlets are covered. Even the most risk-averse toddler can slip and fall or reach out and touch something, and within seconds you can have an emergency on your hands.

When to Call Your Doctor

- High fever (follow your doctor's guidelines)

- Chills that make your toddler shake

- Loss of consciousness

- Extreme sleepiness or unexplained lethargy

- Seizures

- Pain or severe heaviness or stuffiness in the face

- Sudden hysterical crying

- Always call when in doubt

PREPARING FOR TRAVEL

Toddlers need travel routines, even when we are not sure what they will be

Toddlers between 18 and 24 months of age still have no real sense of time, so when we tell them we are going to go to the airport to get on a plane, they become impatient or confused when that does not happen right away. Try to plan travel times that are in sync with your toddler. Since it can take two or more hours from the time you leave for the

airport to actual takeoff, it is usually best to start a trip when your toddler is rested so she does not fall apart too early.

Let your toddler know some of the steps that will happen before you are all in the plane. You can tell him you have to drive to the airport, give your suitcase to a porter, get a boarding pass, and then get on the plane. Once you are at

Tips for Packing

- Start packing a few days ahead of time.

- Know the weather you will likely experience.

- Bring an extra blanket for your toddler at night.

- Bring familiar sippy cups or bottles to help your toddler relax in a new place.

- Bring some socket protectors if you are staying in a hotel room.

- Pack an extra T-shirt for yourself in the diaper bag in case of emergency drips or leaks.

- Keep your toddler's clothes packed in one suitcase for easy access.

Talking about Your Trip

- Do some prep work with your toddler.

- If you are going someplace with different weather, bring pictures of snowmen or beaches. If you are staying at a hotel, talk about the room you will be in and the bed your toddler will

use at night. Explain that his blanket will be with him just like at home.

- Be matter-of-fact, but provide information. Toddlers won't get it all, but they will get enough to help them be better acclimated when you arrive.

the airport, allow your toddler to explore his surroundings. On the plane, some toddlers will be able to settle in pretty quickly, while others will take some time to reset. It is important to have something interactive to distract your toddler at takeoff. Markers that only work on a certain kind of paper are a good option. Also make sure you bring a couple of different kinds of snacks.

ZOOM

Even with the best planning, we cannot guarantee that our toddlers will not cry or yell on the plane. Try to remind yourself that most people are sympathetic, and that those who aren't will have to deal with their own feelings. You can do your best to help your toddler and yourself, but you can't manage the emotions of another person.

Travel Entertainment

- Postpone DVDs until you really need them.

- Interactive sound books are fun, and you can extend the story by looking for farm animals or trucks and cars out the window.

- Pieces of aluminum foil make interesting coloring surfaces for markers or crayons if you are on a plane.

- Oatmeal boxes and animal toys can be a rabbit hole or a house for pigs—a source of creative play.

- If your toddler needs to get down try going to the bathroom for a few minutes and letting him play in the water.

- Bring a puppet to play and be silly with.

Just in Case

- Here are some emergency packable items for you: first-aid kit, including Tylenol and Benadryl, empty plastic bags, extra diapers for a major blowout, small cans of modeling dough for tarmac sitting, big key ring with keys from the hardware store for play, headache medication for you, and a little portable book light so when your toddler falls asleep in your arms, you can read your magazine without the overhead light.

- One more thing: a sense of humor.

FEEDING A TODDLER
Toddler independence versus parent worries can become a focus for mealtimes

Toddlers at this age are developing more self-help skills with eating. They are better able to tell you they are hungry when you ask, and better able to tell you what they want to eat. They enjoy eating with utensils and their hands, and it is difficult as a parent to resist the temptation to feed them, since they can be so messy. It is important to let them feed themselves. Toddlers also are willing to experiment with different foods, especially if they can do it on their own. They continue to model and imitate what they see, so if food is not a positive experience in your family, this is likely to impact your toddler. Try to counteract any negative food impulses you may have.

Popular Toddler Foods

- Toddlers love Popsicles, so try this healthy choice: Mix orange juice and either pineapple or cranberry juice together and freeze. This pop is full of vitamin C, folic acid, and potassium.

- Applesauce mixed with vanilla yogurt is a great dipping sauce for fruit or crackers.

- Mash cooked carrots and a little sour cream to make a great healthy dip for pretzels.

Developing Food Relationships

- Toddlers and parents have different responsibilities when it comes to developing greater independence with eating.

- As gratifying as it may be for us to get our children to eat, this does not allow a child to develop his own relationship with food.

- Self-feeding is a developmental task. Learning to make choices about food preferences, taste, pace, and even the use of utensils helps your toddler develop self-confidence.

Toddler growth slows down after the first year. They continue to want to explore more than eat, so when it is mealtime, try to slow things down and create a relaxing environment free from distractions. Do not pressure your toddler to eat if she is uninterested. Set the food aside and try again in a little while. Toddlers who are pressured into eating are more likely to have worries around food. They will fill up on snacks quite easily, so try to avoid giving snacks an hour before you plan on serving a meal.

There are many cultural differences related to the importance of food and developing greater independence with eating. Your family traditions will help guide you to a place where toddler development and these traditions can intersect most comfortably. When your pediatrician looks at your toddler's growth, make sure she is referencing charts that take into consideration different cultural variations for height and weight.

The Dinner Show

- Modeling good eating habits is probably one of the most important things you can do as a parent. Even if your toddler refuses to try things, he will see you eat foods that are healthy, and over time he will make some of those choices, too.

- Toddlers are curious about what you are eating, even if they are reluctant to try it. They are always paying attention.

Messy Eating

- Toddlers can be messy when they eat. Try not to focus on their hands and faces until dinner is through. They will gain mastery and control with practice and our acceptance.

- If it makes it easier, use an old T-shirt as a bib to make cleanup easier. Toddlers do not like to have their faces washed, but they will be happy to pull a stool over to the sink and clean up themselves.

MORE ON THE FLOOR
Toddlers need food to function, but to them, the function of food is more than just eating

Eighteen- to 24-month-old toddlers can eat almost all of the food you prepare for adult members of the family. If your child has allergies, most of them will have been revealed by this time. Try to plan your meals not just around what your toddler will eat, but also what you like to eat so they can watch you enjoy all kinds of food. If hiding rejected ingredients in

sauces or casseroles works for you, use up some of those leftover jars of baby food and put them in your spaghetti sauce or muffin batter. Most toddlers will eat all kinds of food if they are offered variety from very early on, and parents model open-mindedness.

Remember that toddlers are naturally curious, so try to

Food Power Struggles

- Forcing toddlers to eat can lead to their eating more than they need.

- Power struggles over food tend to leak into other areas of development.

- Arguing over food leads to an increased risk of childhood obesity.

- Help your toddler feel more in control by letting her feed herself. Even if you can only manage this a few times a week, it will help reduce tension over food.

- When you are trying to introduce new foods, also include her favorites.

Eating for Comfort

- When toddlers get tired we often offer them a snack, when what they actually may need is our attention or some quiet time.

- Try offering your toddler water first if she seems to be out of sorts. If this does

not help, see if some one-on-one play time makes a difference.

- If you decide a snack is really what is needed, offer some favorites like colored pasta or a cold sweet potato to dip in yogurt.

serve food in ways that will capture their attention. They can get overwhelmed with portions, so keep theirs very small. Put one or two things on the tray at a time until you see they are interested. This is also a great time to engage toddlers in food preparation, mixing or stirring. They will have a limited attention span, but these are often the times they will stick a finger in a bowl and sample something new.

Being Present

- When you are serving meals to your toddler, sit with him and be engaged. Keep the conversation quiet and positive in tone.

- Toddlers will continue to use their fingers to touch and eat their food. Try

not to rush your toddler through his meals so he has some control.

- Avoid using your phone or watching television, so you can engage in conversation together.

Giving up the High Chair

- When toddlers resist being put in their high chairs, it may be time to switch to a booster seat or small table and chair set.

- When your toddler joins you at the table, she may

want to get up more. If she does, ask her if she is through, and if she is not, remind her to sit back down. If she gets up again she is probably done, so remove her plate and move on.

WHERE DID MY BOTTLE GO?
Toddlers would not choose to give up their bottles, and sometimes neither would we

If toddlers could express what they really think about some of your parenting decisions, giving up the bottle would be a long discussion. Toddlers love their bottles, and so do parents. They are the aces in the hole, the last link that holds us together when our toddlers are falling apart. And then the dentist says, "It's got to go." First things first: You must visualize

how this will play out and prepare yourself. Some toddlers barely blink an eye when the bottle goes, and others refuse milk from a cup altogether. Toddlers will drink milk again, and they will learn coping techniques when the bottle is gone.

Make sure you say good-bye to the bottle on a weekend when you have some time to deal with affected sleep

Calcium Requirements

- Children between one and three need about 500 mg of calcium a day, which is about two glasses of milk.

- Other sources of calcium include sweet potatoes, orange juice, oatmeal, and broccoli.

- Add pureed veggies to batters and sauces if your toddler won't choose these foods on their own.

- For more information, read up on good sources of calcium or locate a nutritionist at one of your area hospitals.

Food Worries

- If your toddler is playing with his food and not eating, he is probably not hungry. Letting go of your worries about his diet are not easy, but prodding and coaxing him to eat will not be helpful in the long run. Toddlers will eat when they are hungry.

- If you have a picky eater, offer smaller meals, or let him help you mix and prepare some food. This can help wet his appetite and even try some bites of food in a relaxed and unpressured way.

routines. Let your toddler know that he will be saying good-bye to the bottle. Eighteen- to 24–month-old toddlers understand more than they can actually express, so be honest about what is going to happen. Use baby dolls to practice nighttime routines without the bottle. Put the bottles in a shoebox together, and put the box in the closet. Make sure you say good-bye together. If your toddler cries, this is a great time to help with some emotion coaching.

Say Cheese

- Take pictures of your toddler eating at the table or in his high chair and make a book about mealtimes.

- Let him describe what he sees in the pictures. Make this a fun activity to show that mealtimes do not have to be about discord between the two of you.

- During mealtime try to focus on the day, the upcoming activities. and what you will do after you eat. This can take the pressure off the meal.

Hello, Anyone Out There?

- Finding support for yourself may be useful if you are at your wit's end.

- Try a "webininar" or online seminar, where you can join online interactive nutrition presentations on helping your toddler learn how to eat and learning how to let go of power struggles.

- Try to think about your own food struggles and see if some of your own worries are mixing into feeding your toddler.

HUNGER STRIKES
Dear Diary, day three—still barely a bite

Toddlers, unlike most adults, go through periods where they are just not that into food. In fact, unless they are sick and not eating, toddlers may have two or three days at a time where they barely eat at all. They seem to be energetic and happy but just not interested in sitting still long enough to eat. Make sure that food does not become a power struggle, even if you are concerned. Try offering some fruity shakes,

and let your toddler help cut up the fruit. This sometimes reactivates the taste buds. Don't be afraid to serve the same thing three times a day if there are only one or two things she will eat during this period.

Eighteen- to 24-month-old toddlers are getting clearer about their food preferences, and you can begin to ask them what they would like to eat. It is important just to offer two

Hunger Strikes

- There are many factors that can contribute to toddler hunger strikes. Headaches and sore gums, teeth, or ears are all reasons why a toddler will not eat.

- Sometimes the symptoms are not obvious, and refusing food may be his way of letting you know something is wrong. If your toddler continues to refuse food, check with your pediatrician.

Naming the Feeling

- When a toddler has a minor sore throat or some gum discomfort one day and is not eating, he may be hesitant to eat much the next day even if his mouth feels better. Toddlers are cautious if they have experienced discomfort.

- Name your toddler's experience. Talk to him about how his teeth hurt yesterday, but explain that today they may be just fine. Encourage him to try again, but don't force him.

things, as toddlers cannot choose between a larger number. If they say no to everything, reoffer later on. If they are not eating much, toddlers will often ask for more liquids, so let them drink more milk or juice until they are ready to start eating again. Unless there is some unlikely underlying issue, they will.

Is He Starving?

- When a toddler is going though a period of not eating, we worry about nutrition. Toddlers will not starve themselves. Give them time.

- You may have to wet your toddler's taste buds a little, so try a favorite. Keep a few homemade juice pops in the freezer and serve one with dinner. They are easy to make, pour, and freeze.

Ambience

- Sometimes toddlers need help setting the mood for food, especially if they are in a picky place.

- Try reading some great food books. The Very Hungry Caterpillar and Jamberry make food look delicious and interesting. When you serve lunch, you can ask your toddler if she remembers what the caterpillar ate.

FAMILY TIMES STILL IMPORTANT

No matter what age toddler you have, finding time for family meals is still very important

Continuing to develop family mealtimes and rituals is important. As children grow older, they will come to count on these traditions and use mealtimes as an important venue for coming together and engaging in discussions, learning new things, and developing deeper connections with family. Try to set up this expectation realistically. Regular family mealtimes usually work best if there are no time pressures for anyone. If there are time constraints, it is still worth trying to sit together for a short meal, rather than eating separately at different times. Try not to focus on the food as much as the experience of being together. Continue to use some way of beginning and ending your meal to mark the difference

Family Meal Benefits

- Give you an opportunity to set aside anger or frustration

- Create a safe space for talking and sharing

- Increase humor and silliness

- Develop closeness and connection

- Promote your family values and beliefs

Modeling After Siblings

- Toddlers often eat better when they are sitting with their siblings. They may try different foods and enjoy getting help from their big brother or sister.

- This is a good time to establish a noncompetitive environment. Try not to point out what one child is eating to another. This kind of competition will just increase rivalry in other areas.

between this meal and the other times your toddler eats.

Family mealtimes do not have to mean elaborate or time-consuming cooking or preparation. Whatever solution creates the least stress in the meal provider is the best one. A take-out order or bowls of cereal and fruit will do just fine. It is the ritual and meaning you all create together that will leave your children with a lasting message.

Tell your toddler that it is family mealtime beforehand so she can begin to see the predictable pattern each day. When mealtime is over, try to transition together so the pleasure of the time is not just cut off as everyone goes off to do his own thing. You may decide that you will wash dishes together or take out the garbage. For a toddler, this is not work yet. It is about being together and feeling connected, and toddlers love to be included in family activities.

Starting the Day

- Morning time can be stressful when there is a lot of activity. Some toddlers actually eat better when they are watching all the action, and some just get overwhelmed.

- If you have to get out of the house quickly, family mealtime may have to be taken on the road. Make the most of it when it happens by creating a traveling picnic. Toasted cheese sandwiches to go are fast and fun.

Fancy Meals

- If you occasionally enjoy a more formal mealtime, set some traditions your toddler will recognize each time. Light candles; put on a tablecloth.

- When you have a young toddler, it may be easier to do these mealtimes earlier so she does not fall apart before the wine or chocolate milk is poured. If you need to do it later because of work schedules, bathe your toddler earlier so she can still come to the first part of the meal.

FOOD ALLERGIES

Food allergies are serious and play a significant role in a family's life

Food allergies are very real, and it is important to discuss your own health history with your pediatrician before you start your baby on solid foods. Your doctor may decide to delay introducing certain foods such as eggs, dairy, tree nuts, or peanuts depending on your experiences. Make sure that when you add potentially troublesome foods that you go slowly and monitor reactions carefully.

There are many food allergy myths to be aware of. Children can be lactose intolerant or have a certain food aversion that leaves them gassy or uncomfortable rather than an actual allergy. Let your doctor know exactly what happens if your child has a reaction. Toddlers may get very fussy after eating something that is not comfortable for them to digest. Your doctor can do blood tests to determine whether your child has food allergies.

Planning for School

Allergy Information Web Sites

- Food Allergy Initiative —tips for managing food allergies at home, school, and camp and great restaurant cards.
  www.faiusa.org

- Food Allergy and Anaphylaxis Network— latest information on allergies, product recalls, and children's allergy books.
  www.foodallergy.org

- Kids with Food Allergies—links to allergy articles and research.
  www.kidswithfoodallergies.org

- Food allergy Web site just for kids— coloring projects and activities.
  www.faankids.org

- Allergy Haven—recommended books.
  www.allergyhaven.com

- There are many ways you can customize your toddler's food containers to make sure her food is clearly marked when she attends school.

- There are allergy stickers, lunch bags, and even brace-

lets your toddler can wear if she has a life-threatening allergy.

- Ask your toddler's school or day care if they have a plan in place, or see if they will let you write one to use in the classroom.

Although there are foods that toddlers are more likely to be allergic to, all foods, including fruits and vegetables, can trigger allergic responses. About 80 percent of children will outgrow allergies if allergenic foods are eliminated from their diet initially. It is important to note that reactions can vary from day to day, and if your toddler has only a minor reaction to a food one time, he could have a severe reaction the next. If your toddler has an adverse reaction to a food, it must be taken very seriously. It is essential that you find a doctor who specializes in food allergies for young children. Pediatric allergists are an excellent source of information and can help calm you down when you are worried about your toddler's eating challenges. Many pediatricians offer support groups for parents of children with allergies. These groups can be very helpful if you are feeling isolated and frustrated with your child's allergies.

Sweet Alternatives

- Children love sweets, and there are companies that specialize in safe desserts and treats.

- Families who have experienced challenges with their own children and decided to create safe and inviting alternatives have started most of these companies. Take a look, but always check ingredients yourself.

Testing for Allergies

- There are a number of ways you can have your toddler checked for allergies. The prick test is most commonly used. Skin testing is done by placing drops of common allergens on your child's skin and having the doctor observe reactions. Light pricks are then made in the skin for further observation.

- Consult with your pediatrician to find out what the next steps are when you suspect allergies.

TODDLER PLAY IS CHANGING
Complicated themes and toddler reasoning are becoming part of toddler play

Between 18 and 24 months, toddler play is taking a significant turn. There is much greater awareness of cause and effect, and repetition is much more intentional. Toddlers also begin to understand humor in very simple ways. A joke to a toddler is a box on your head that falls off. They begin to see these types of interaction as playful, which is different than play that is more purposeful.

Toddlers still continue to do solitary play, but at times move a little closer to the action of other children with parallel play. You will see toddlers using materials to mirror what they see you do. They will take a block and use it as a phone or remote control. They are determined to figure things out without

How the Brain Learns 101

- The brain has many regions that control specific functions, such as thinking, reasoning, language, and emotions.

- At birth a baby's brain has millions of connecting neurons.

- When new information comes in through the senses, neurons make connections of understanding.

- The neurons are connecting continuously as babies experience stimuli and messages are sent through these pathways.

- The number and organization of connections influence everything from learning the alphabet to social skills.

- Some neurons are pruned through life, but the ones that are meaningful stay and even increase.

Connecting Brain Paths

- Whether our children play randomly or purposefully, the neuron connectors are strengthened. The brain is constantly seeking new information that helps shape a toddler's intellectual, social, and emotional development.

- The brain is always trying to understand patterns, so consistency whenever possible helps toddlers build foundational skills for later academic success.

any interference from you. One of the challenges we have as parents is keeping up with the pace of the play.

Toddlers move quickly and seek new things, including objects that are not meant as toys. Parents need to decide whether they will put away breakable things or teach their toddlers not to touch. Remember that toddlers need to be persistent to master the challenges of the world they are living in. At this age, they are not intentionally doing things to irritate or upset you.

Playing Outside

- When children play outside, they develop a greater sense of the bigger world. They see how other children play and how other adults behave. Your toddler is observing and comparing this information to her own experiences.

- Outdoor play also exercises problem-solving because it engages more muscles, helping toddlers gain more mastery of coordination and agility.

Toddlers Imitate Everything

- Toddlers are fascinated with other children. Frequently, you see the results of parallel play in the days that follow, when your toddler is trying to practice what he has observed.

- Of course, not everything he has observed is positive, so you will need to watch carefully. Say, "I know James put that in his mouth, and remember, his mom said no too." This connects the past to present for him. It is a great brain exercise!

18–24 MO.: PLAY

PARALLEL PLAY

As play changes, so do your toddler's skills and understanding of the world

Play stages are not discreet stages. They all blend together, as toddlers use their natural scientific curiosity to understand their relationships to objects and people. As toddlers learn about objects, they try to transfer the information they have to see if humans work the same way. Humans are much more unpredictable, though, and a group of children can be busy, loud, and sometimes full of conflict. Toddlers at this age will watch other children play to engage not with them, but with the materials they are using. Toddlers are not wired yet to share. They cannot relate to another child's feelings, as they do not even understand their own. Eighteen- to 24-month-old toddlers are still very sensory

Creating Play Setups

- Create play setups using what you have. These setups define space and offer new concepts.

- Lay out a blue sheet and put all your toddler's stuffed or plastic fish-related toys together for a swim in the ocean.

- Set up a corner with cardboard blocks and stuffed penguins for a giant iceberg.

- Lay out a green sheet and put all of your toddler's green toys on it.

- Lay out a white sheet and put lots of pillows on it.

Toddler Connections

- Although toddlers engage in parallel play most of the time, some will attempt to cross over. Toddlers will even experience shared humor with a peer. If one of them starts to run and laugh, the other will join in, and they will have a few moments of recognizing shared pleasure and connection.

- This is a big deal in toddler play and brain development. Use some words to strengthen the connection. Say, "You and Ethan really like to run together."

motor oriented. They want to know: Can I eat it, smell it, touch it, or move it?

Parallel play is partly about experiencing a commonality, realizing that desires can be shared. It is the beginning of moral development—crude but critical. Toddlers are acquiring a sense of right and wrong as they watch another child cry or yell when a toy is snatched away. This increased self-awareness helps toddlers differentiate themselves from others, with realizations such as, "Max loves the truck, but I am just not that into it."

Recognizing Parallel Play

- Parallel play at the park can sometimes be hard to recognize if there is a lot going on.

- Your toddler may be interacting with another child who leaves quickly to pursue another activity. This can keep things moving fast and at times can be confusing for a child.

- Toddlers need more descriptive language from adults to help sort out what they are seeing. Say, "I know you were jumping with Megan, and then she left and ran with Charlie."

Monkey See, Monkey Do

- Behaviors are contagious, so a friend who has nibbled on another friend can start a wave of biting in a group. Toddler biting is painful but not at all unusual. This is small consolation, but biting behavior should pass in about six weeks.

- Your toddler will need help with limit setting and other ways to soothe himself if frustrated or teething. Biting back or spanking models the behavior you are trying to extinguish, so use a gentle removal and no biting words.

TOYS, TOYS, TOYS
Anything and everything is a toddler toy

One of the keys to toddler toy success is having multiples. Toddlers love piles of balls: big, small, plain, and patterned. Filling up a laundry basket with balls and then dumping it out can hold a toddler's attention for up to five minutes. That may not seem like a long time to you yet, but the more time you spend with a toddler, the more you will value those five-minute chunks of time. Large boxes that

hold balls or other objects are also important. Not only can toddlers climb in and out of them, but you can introduce a concept called scaffolding, or a bridge to more complex play.

When your toddler is in the box, ask him if he wants to drive the car. Hand him some play keys, make an engine noise, and wave good-bye. You have now opened up a world of pretend

Must-Haves for Play

- Selection of different songs and sounds on your iPod, from drumming rhythms to classical

- Musical garden of instruments for toddler to explore

- Large-knobbed puzzles for toddler to begin to understand spatial relationships

- Large drawing pads and big, chunky crayons

- Large cardboard blocks—easy to assemble and great for building and dramatic play

- Large paintbrushes so toddler can paint with a bucket of water—can be done indoors on windows, or outdoors on anything

- Garage, castle, or house play set with people

Imaginary Play Worlds

- By 24 months, toddlers are becoming more interested in dramatic or pretend play. They are able to follow a simple story line with your help and add ideas and elements of their own.

- This is a good time to mix things like building

blocks and plastic animals together to create a farm or a zoo. Try to let your toddler have control over the construction no matter how good an idea you have for the barn.

through your engagement and the simple act of combining some toys.

Toddlers need to have music all around them. Put out some small drums, a little keyboard, some spoons to bang, and some big bells. When they shake their instruments, dance and sing, and let them explore the sounds. If it is hard for you to tolerate a lot of noise, try to pick just one time a day when these instruments are out. Sometimes it helps if you put on some background music for yourself. At first, your toddler may look at the instruments, or chew on a few, but after a while you can do some more scaffolding and help her feel more connected to a musical experience of interaction, sound, and pleasure. When children are surrounded by art and music as part of their toy world, they will begin to play more creatively in a natural way.

Some Toddlers Don't Like Mess

- Not all toddlers like to get their hands messy. If your toddler is more sensitive about touching things, let her explore textures in her own time with some encouragement along the way.

- Your toddler may be okay touching the paint for a second with one finger, but then need to have it wiped off. Tell her you saw her try, and be as matter-of-fact as possible. Praise can have the unintended effect of creating resistance.

Moving Is Natural

- Toddlers love to dance and move. Practice stopping and starting to music or spinning, which they can do without feeling dizzy or ill. They will find a rhythm or beat to the music when you offer lots of opportunities.

- This is a good time to load your iPod with a variety of music: slow, fast, marching, beat, reggae, or whatever you like. Some toddlers love to have you put bells on their feet to hear how their movements sound.

BOOKS OPEN NEW WORLDS

As your toddler begins to develop more language, books can be used to tell simple stories

Books are another way to help scaffold the world for your 18- to 24-month-old toddler. With books you can begin to look at themes and find simple stories that introduce new vocabulary and reflect the many experiences a toddler is now having in her day. Toddlers can retain more of a story now and help retell it. The experience of reading to your toddler becomes more enjoyable as she begins to select favorite books or look for favorite characters. Many toddler books can be sung, which can enhance your toddler's engagement with the story. Try to set up story times that are separate from bedtime. This allows your child an opportunity to be more interactive with the book.

More Involved Storylines

- Reading for many toddlers becomes more and more engaging, especially if the experience is relaxing for both of you.

- Toddlers often like the same story over and over. This will change, but now the familiar is important to them.

- Try planning a reading time with your toddler other than bedtime. If she is giving up a morning nap, this can be a nice replacement activity to recharge both of you.

Great Toddler Books

Toddlers now like books that have a short storyline and reflect some of what they are experiencing. Here are a few that are often a hit:

- Sheep in the Jeep by Margot Apple
- We Are Going on a Bear Hunt by Michael Rosen and Helen Oxenbury
- Where's My Teddy? by Jez Alborough
- Counting Kisses by Karen Katz
- Freight Train by Donald Crews
- Happy Egg by Ruth Krauss
- Napping House by Audrey Wood
- Toolbox by Tomi diPaola

114

You can also use a story to facilitate play. For example, after you have read the *Bear Hunt* book, hide your toddler's stuffed bears and look for them together. This not only deepens the meaning, but also underscores the language in the story. You can also use books to introduce upcoming events and to prepare your toddler for a new experience, such as a plane ride or the first day of day care. The best stories for toddlers help them make sense of their inner world of emotions.

Comparing to Others

- Story time may start to smooth out during this age range, but it is rarely consistent. When you find yourself comparing your toddler to someone else's, remind yourself that your child will get to a place where she is comfortable.

- If your toddler won't sit or is always turning the other way, try to accept where she is. It will change, and when you can accept where she is in her journey, she will be able to get where you would like her to be.

Highlight Book Options

- Toddlers will start to seek out books on their own during this stage. They will pause, flip a page, or just look at the cover for a while. Try setting out a small blanket and highlighting a couple of books on it each day.

- Watch your toddler notice what you set up and then go over to look at the books. Brains are novelty seeking, and these setups strike toddlers with much interest.

PLAY IS HARD WORK

Play requires us to suspend our logical minds and to think like toddlers

For many adults, play is hard. It requires allowing a toddler to determine the rules. We may want to build a tall tower, when our toddler wants is to knock it down. We may want to race a car down a ramp, when our toddler just wants to put the car in the elevator. Toddlers need leadership experience because most of the time they are in the backseat while we are driving their daily schedule. Playing with toddlers allows them to have power in a safe way and allows us to get attuned to them.

Attuning to your 18- to 24-month-old toddler is like learning how your car handles. After miles of experience on the road, you know when to go fast, when to go slow, and when

Roughhousing Is Important

- Toddlers go through periods where they will want either more or less rough-and-tumble play. When this happens, try to let him make that choice without influencing him with your preferences.

- Sometimes if toddlers have been very overstimulated from roughhousing the day before, they are reluctant to enter into it again without knowing they will have some control. Ask him if he would like to bounce a little today. Try to respect his words.

Set Goals for Playtime

- Sometimes mothers will express that they do not have the luxury their partners do to play because of the many responsibilities they have. If you find yourself saying this, it is time to figure out how to give yourself 30 minutes a day to play.

- Sometimes parents are reluctant to play because it can feel too open-ended and without a purpose or goal. Try in these moments to remember that play helps your toddler learn social skills through trial and error.

to change the oil. If you don't pay attention to cues, your car breaks down. Act out rituals with your toddler, make time for pretend play, and be silly. Make believe you are cooking dinner for each other or filling up your car with gas; pretend you cannot find your keys and act surprised when your toddler gives them to you. All of these experiences are ways for your toddler to learn how to interact in relationships.

ZOOM

When you play with your toddler, try not to be distracted by the outside world. A study done at Harvard University showed that babies as young as six months old became fussy and irritable when their parents took out their cell phones. When you focus on your toddler for 20 to 30 minutes a day and play, the message you send is crucial: Your toddler matters.

Sibling Play

- Sibling play is complicated. Toddlers are more familiar with their siblings than their friends, so they may be more persistent.

- Sibling play usually needs a parent close by. If things start to fall apart, sometimes just sitting down with them for five minutes without saying anything about the struggle can help to shift the energy.

- If your children are fighting, try to avoid pointing out who is big or little and just focus on helping each of them move on to something else.

Focused Playtime

- Make floor time a priority.

- Sometimes snack or lunch time may be the only time you have that day, but take advantage of it.

- Engage with your toddler in open communication. Say, "I can see you were thirsty. You drank a lot of juice." Let her weigh in: She may say yes or just listen. Pause and give her time to react or respond.

- When you are there, the eye contact in that moment may be more important than the verbal connection.

117

PARENTS PLAY DIFFERENTLY

Men and women have different goals when playing with their children

Playing with babies and toddlers looks very different depending on who is doing the play. Dads tend to be more active, more playful, and more able to generate lots of energy and positive play experiences with their children. Extensive research tells us that there are long-term benefits from fathers' playing in a more active, rough-and-tumble way with toddlers.

Fathers send a message that exploring is good and give children opportunities to learn about self-control and starting and stopping. All of these skills have been shown to improve peer relationships later on in school. Of course, you have to be present emotionally to play, and it is essential for both mothers and fathers to model empathy and caring. Moms and

How Dads and Moms Play

- Our children are learning important things by learning differences. Dads and moms do things differently and that is okay, as long as the general goals you have agreed on stay the same, such as the time for lights out.

- If bedtime rituals are different when your partner does them, just remember it is about the end goal: sleep. Don't interfere. If things do not go well, partners will self-correct as needed.

Modeling Problem-Solving

- Children need to see parents problem-solve. This does not mean that both of you have to know how to fix every problem, but that each of you models ways to break down problems and find solutions.

- Toddlers will observe how you handle these differences between you, so avoid blame or contempt when you are disagreeing.

dads do this differently, but it is the mix of styles that provides toddlers with an early look at gender differences.

Even when we try to be gender neutral, we see toy preferences early on with young children that seem gender specific. It is good to provide a mixture of all kinds of toys for your child, but even if your son will have nothing to do with a baby doll, he can still learn similar lessons from playing with a car. The object is different, but the goals are the same. Your toddler is learning how things work and how to take care of something he loves.

During their toddler years, boys and girls are learning to differentiate themselves, which means gender identification. This is more than knowing who has what parts; it is also understanding what makes up the differences. Allowing your toddler to develop a different relationship with each parent is critical. It is the early modeling of relationships between parents and children that provides opportunities for healthy intimacy later on in life.

Nurturing across Party Lines

- Toddlers need to see nurturing dads as well as moms. Make sure both of you have time alone with your toddler to run errands or be in the house together. This allows each of you to provide comfort and help when the other parent is not around.

- Toddlers need to hear they are loved, so don't hold back.

Out of Your Comfort Zone

- Sometimes it is harder for a dad to play dolls or a mom to play with cars. If that is the case, observe how the other parent does it. You won't be able to do it in the exact same way, but you will pick up tips.

- It is good for children to see us using their playthings comfortably and without too much outward or spoken bias.

TODDLERS REALLY DO CONNECT

At around 18 months, toddlers start to make meaningful connections with familiar people

Toddlers between 18 and 24 months of age begin to recognize significant people in their lives. Grandparents, babysitters, and friends start to play important roles in your toddler's world. They are now able to hold memories, so they can recall what they did with grandma last week, or even last month, if you help them keep the memory alive. Toddlers are also able to understand that when a sitter arrives, you leave, so don't be surprised if they become clingier. It will take different toddlers different amounts of time to transition to new social situations. Some will move quickly to engage with a familiar person, while others will take their time, stay close to you, and slowly allow themselves to be engaged.

Social Connections

- Toddlers can now remember what happens, so talk about upcoming social engagements.

- Allow your toddler some space to get comfortable.

- Be open—different days bring different responses.

- Remind yourself that different temperaments require different reactions from you.

Sibling Connections

- School age siblings may make more room for a toddler then a preschooler.

- Preschoolers are still in the throes of learning turn-taking, so they may struggle to find a balance with their younger brother or sister. This can be tense for parents because the conflicts can be steady.

- Try to remind yourself this is finite, and do not expect your older child to make it all right for all of you.

Toddler social behavior may seem confusing at times. They are trying to get some solid footing before they allow themselves to enter a social connection emotionally. This is where social modeling and emotion coaching can be very helpful. Give your toddler some time to observe a situation, remind her of what happened the last time she was in this situation, and tell her she can stay close until she's ready to get down and play. It is important to remind grandparents, who may be very eager to reconnect, to avoid moving in too quickly.

●●●●●●●●●● GREEN ● LIGHT ●●●●●●●●●●

Talking to in-laws can be difficult. Try saying to your toddler, "Do you remember that when Grandma comes she likes to hold you right away and give you kisses? Some people go slow, and some people go fast—Grandma goes so fast." This helps your toddler understand the meaning of the greeting and do some preparing. It still may not go smoothly, but it gives both of you some language.

Underfoot and Everywhere

- Toddlers want to do what you do much of the time. If you run the vacuum, they are right there; if you need to grab the mail, they are underfoot. The desire to stay close and imitate what you do intensifies around 18 months.

- Your toddler may be saying, "I need some attention." Ten minutes of floor time can lighten the mood. If she is persistent, use a timer to take turns. Once she knows she can do what you're doing, she will likely move on to something else.

Healing Relationships

- Grandparents can play an important role in your family.

- Behaviors from your parents may surprise you.

- Often, as grandparents they are able to act differently than they did when they were parents. You may have felt your dad was never around, yet now he seems to always have time to play with your child.

- Doing the best you can as a parent looks different at different stages of our lives. This awareness can bring healing in your own parent relationships.

GROUP THINK

Toddlers are amazingly observant, so be prepared for some imitating when you least expect it

Toddlers in groups are like bumper cars—they collide to see what will happen next. They are trying to understand how they fit into a group. Our parental expectations change dramatically as our toddlers change and grow, complicating things. We now hope they can control their impulses, follow rules and directions, and shine—all at the same time. We tell ourselves that we are going with the flow and letting our toddlers learn by trial and error, but, of course, we want play-dates and classes to go smoothly.

When you bring your toddler into a group situation, make sure that the facilitators where you are going are experienced with toddler behaviors. A group where toddlers have to

Organized Open Play

- Toddlers still need very few, if any, directed group activities. The goal of these classes is to have fun and expose your toddler to new things.

- Parents often say they want their children to learn to be social and that they feel pressured to accomplish it in a class.

- Being social is a lifelong lesson: Baby steps at first, and for many toddlers just being in the same room as 10 other children is a big effort for them.

Finding Good Child Care

- Day care continues to be controversial. But the research is pretty clear: Good, responsive care has no negative impact on toddlers.

- Responsive care is the most important part of a toddler's world, whether at home or in a separate setting. The challenge is finding care you can afford and is high quality. Local agencies can help you select a program.

- Your toddler will take about six weeks to adjust because he is trying to separate and experience all new things.

participate for more than 5 or 10 minutes may not work. You may end up chasing them around, keeping them occupied with food, or holding them at the door. Talk with the leader of the group beforehand to learn what is expected of you and your toddler. If he is hit or bitten or is a hitter, ask how to best handle this in a group setting. These are not unusual behaviors for toddlers, and many will experiment with one or more. It is just that we do not usually see our toddlers do these things at home, so they stand out more in group settings.

These behaviors are not indicators of developmental delays or poor parenting, so take your time, take a deep breath, and take some comfort knowing that your toddler will change as he understands other ways to act on his feelings. Try not to worry about what other parents are thinking. Remember: You are all in the same boat.

DIY Mommy and Me

- If you cannot find a mommy-and-me class that is affordable or works with your schedule, try putting together something yourself.

- Invite two or three other moms over and take turns planning an easy activity:

sing a song, have a snack together, and let the toddlers play. Keep it short and simple.

- Rotating houses is sometimes easier and limits cleanup. Try doing it once a week for a month and see how it goes.

Play Groups

Successful play groups

- give toddlers time to explore;

- are not too stimulating;

- are not too loud;

- provide safe physical environments to move around in;

- have clear routines for toddlers to understand.

HELPING TODDLERS PLAY
Even play is something we learn how to do

When toddlers are in a room together, they need help learning how to begin and end interactions. Try to keep your goals simple for your child. If toddlers can be next to each other for short periods of time, they will be able to see how other children play and use materials.

When toddlers first enter a space with other children, they need time to roam around. They will move from toy to toy,

looking, touching, and sometimes grabbing from each other. If this happens, it is tempting to pull the toy away from the child that grabs, especially if it is your own. Try to resist. You want your toddler to learn social skills. If you pull, the only skill they will learn is to keep imitating you. Instead, try to exchange with them. If that does not work and the other child is still interested in what she has lost, begin emotion coaching.

Helping Toddlers Relax

- Relaxing is most effective for toddlers when we have our feelings under control.

- Toddlers do not look the way we do when we are relaxed because they prefer movement to stillness.

- They relax when we are matter-of-fact about what is going on.

- Toddlers can relax when they feel there is emotional space for them. If they feel worried or anxious about your reactions, they will not relax as much.

Setting the Stage

- When you want to encourage your toddler to do some quieter things, it will most likely have to start with you. Try setting the stage.

- If your toddler is running around and you need her

to slow down for a while, spread a blanket on the floor—she will pause to watch. Go get her puzzles, and sit down and begin to play with them. In most cases, your toddler will be over in a wink before you have even uttered a word.

There is a tremendous amount of repetition at this age, when toddlers are learning new skills. The challenge with social skills is that the pay-off for a toddler is actually learning how to defer gratification, which is a very difficult concept to teach.

·········· **GREEN ● LIGHT** ··············

If your toddler grabs a toy from another child, say, "I know you want that toy. Emily had it first, so I will find something else for you." Pick up your toddler and look for something else together without taking the toy from her. When you find something of interest, take her to give Emily back the toy. Remind yourself that the foundation you set now will pay off big-time later on.

Short Breaks

- Toddlers can play alone for five minutes, give or take a few, and this may be the total time they are content over a two- or three-hour period. If you are counting on this time to accomplish something, even a bathroom trip, you will be frustrated.

- Try to find a sitter or neighbor child (12-year-olds are pretty good at this when you are also around) who can be there with your toddler for an hour while you finish getting ready for company or take a quick shower.

Slow to Warm

- It can be hard to watch another child join an activity, while your child clings to you.

- Some children are just slow to warm up, and no amount of coaxing will change that. Let them have some space.

- If you try to engage your toddler so you can step back, he will not trust you the next time. Let him know you will stay close and tell him if you want to go to the bathroom or sit down.

- It may take many group situations before he is able to regulate his feelings.

HELLOS & GOOD-BYES

Hellos and good-byes are a real challenge for parents, because greetings and departures tug at our own heartstrings

Part of the reason it is so hard for toddlers to say good-bye is because they have to leave the loves of their lives: you. When you are gone, they now have the cognitive memory to realize it and miss you. Their lack of ambivalence is countered by your ambivalence at times: It is hard to leave you, too, but I need a break.

When it is time to separate, there are some really important things you can do to help your toddler. First, let him know where you are going. Remember, he may not have a lot of speaking language, but he has a lot of receptive, or understood, language. When you leave, make sure you say good-bye, which may be hard for two reasons: The person you are

Trust and Follow-through

- The most important emotional and social skills you can pass on to your child are trust and follow-through.

- Say to your toddler, "I will always tell you what is really happening, and you can always count on me." When children know this, they will believe you when you tell them, "I will be back in a little while," or, "You will feel much better after a few minutes."

Leaving You

- For many toddlers, it is easier to leave you than to be left.

- If you are going out during the day, have your caregiver take your toddler to the park. Say good-bye to her, but make sure you still tell her that you will be going out while she is away.

leaving your toddler with may tell you it is easier if you just slip out because he is happily playing, or your toddler may be crying.

Explain to your sitter that you will be telling your toddler you are going to leave. Ask her to think of ways she can help him settle down if he gets very upset, and let her know that it will get easier.

ZOOM

During these first years of developing social skills, your toddler may express a preference for you over your partner or vice versa. It is hard for toddlers to know what to do with all of their affection. She is also now aware that she has different relationships with each of you and may want to experiment with how these relationships work. It is important that you do your best not to take it personally.

Primary Teachers

- If your toddler is enrolled in a child-care setting while you work, ask for a primary teacher to oversee his care.

- A primary teacher can help with the good-byes and transition your toddler to the routine of the day. This continuity of caregiving helps minimize the stress toddlers can sometimes experience when you leave to go off to work. This teacher can also provide details about your toddler's day.

Transitions at School

- Teachers sometimes say, "She is fine once you go." For some toddlers this is close to their experience, but for others how they feel on the inside may be different from how they look. Ask the teachers what emotional support they provide to help your toddler with her feelings.

- If your toddler cries, say, "I think you are having a missing feeling. I will miss you too. Remember the other day when you had a good time building with your teacher?" You are helping your child see that she can have more than one feeling about school.

TODDLER TALK

Toddlers need help developing friendships and knowing that not all friends are equal

With playdates, it is important to help your toddler make connections in an age-appropriate way. Having a comfortable connection with the other parent is helpful. You need to feel that you and your toddler are both at ease.

You may find it easier at first to go to someone else's house, so you can leave when you're ready. If the play is going well,

try not to stay much longer than an hour; you want to end on an up note. When play is falling apart, stay for 30 minutes and then let the toddlers know they will be able to try another day.

Toddlers can be very territorial and have a hard time sharing their belongings, including you. Their behavior is not a

Playdates

- Playdates should still be short—try limiting them to an hour.

- Try to have the first part of a playdate with both you and the other parent engaged on the floor. When your toddlers begin to feel comfortable, they will start to move away from you more easily.

- Leave when it is still positive. It is tempting to have playdates to enjoy adult companionship, but this may need to wait until you see your toddlers are able to manage the time.

Hosting Another Toddler

- When another toddler comes to your house, try not to assume she will be of the same temperament as your toddler. She may be more or less active, or more or less easily frustrated.

- Unless you are close friends with the other toddler's par-

ents, it can be very uncomfortable managing your reactions to her behavior. Sometimes a quick phone call to the other parent the day before a playdate can help, so the two of you can have a greater comfort level with each other.

predictor of future social skills, just a reflection of where they are right now. Try sitting down on the floor with the two toddlers. Start a game and let each one have some time to react or engage. After a few minutes they often attempt to advance the game by taking away or holding one of the objects. Encourage this, and name the actions. Say, "Looks like Megan found the ball." When they are done, stay down and let them come to you. This allows them some safety as they move around and explore.

Toddler Manners

- Introduce manners. Since toddlers are concrete thinkers, keep it short and sweet. Say, "Manners are special words that make us feel good. If I give your bear a cookie, he will feel good and so will I, so we say 'please' and 'thank-you.'"

- Decide with your partner what manners you will start with.

- Model: Toddlers learn best through imitation.

- If your toddler refuses to say "please," try saying: "Maybe you can try again in a moment because I want you to have your cookie."

- Don't humiliate or embarrass him—that is not good manners.

Providing Language

- Toddlers speak to adults faster than to their peers. They learn quickly that adults can understand them better and get them what they need and want.

- You can encourage language between toddlers by saying, "Try telling Graham you want that." Your toddler does not have to say the words, but you are giving her language to use when she is ready.

PREGNANCY & TODDLERS
Pregnancy can be difficult when you have a busy toddler

There are different challenges when we become pregnant for the second time, regardless of the age of your first child. If you have a toddler, finding time to rest or relax is certainly one of these challenges. Toddlers are busy by their very nature, and explaining that you are having a baby means nothing more than saying you are buying a new sports car.

As you approach your due date, it becomes more difficult to be physical with your toddler. Try to put a mat on the floor and sit next to him, so if he wants to climb on your lap, you are a little more accessible. When your toddler wants to be picked up, try kneeling and holding him in your arms. If he will not accept this as an alternative, have him climb on a stool and try from a standing position.

Something Is Changing

- Once you begin to show, your toddler will notice something is changing. When you see her looking at your belly, give her words. Say, "I think you just saw how my belly is getting big. This is where our baby is living until he is ready to come out here with us."

- Many children are reluctant to touch your stomach during the end of the pregnancy. They are not rejecting you, just trying to understand what has changed.

Rest Together

- Try resting with your toddler if she is still napping or taking a quiet time in her room. Now you have to take what you can get.

- You cannot store sleep, but try to be as rested as you

can. Go to sleep earlier at night, lay down on weekends, nap, and use a sitter once in a while to take your toddler to the park so you can sleep or rest.

While all these different moves are being adopted, keep using descriptive language with your toddler so he has an explanation, even if it is not a satisfactory one. Keep the explanation focused on your body, not the new baby. Your toddler can see you are changing, so the narrative will make more concrete sense. Toddlers are definitely cause-and-effect driven.

Preparing for the Baby

- Because of the height of your toddler, your new baby can hear her voice very well. After birth, babies track to the sound of their sibling within a few seconds.

- Begin to wonder out loud to your toddler what this baby will look like. Show her baby pictures.

- Toddlers often become more upset about separating from you at the end of the pregnancy. They are aware that something feels different so give them some feeling words to help them understand.

Staying Healthy Together

- Try exercising with your toddler as an active way to get ready for the baby. Talk about how good it feels to be strong.

- Lay down on mats together, stretch, do some yoga pretzels together, drink water. Talk about how nice it is to get ready together for the new baby.

COGNITIVE DEVELOPMENT

This is a rich, interwoven mix of many areas of toddler development

Toddlers between 24 and 36 months of age are constructing more and more elaborate themes and ways of understanding the world. They can say more, understand more, recognize patterns, and have clearer intentions of what they would like and how they are going to get it.

Toddlers can now take a puzzle or shape sorter, quickly drop in a piece, and move on. They no longer have to explore each piece by taste or sound, and can remember the meaning of the toy and how to use it. They are also able to predict what happens when you open a certain cupboard where their cookies are, even if it is 7:00 in the morning. Toddlers can think ahead, remember, and wonder what will happen next but still cannot distinguish yesterday from today or tomorrow.

Seeing the Wheels Turn

Cognitive Development

At 24 to 36 months toddlers are getting cognitively better at:

- Remembering events

- Expressing thoughts and ideas

- Recalling patterns and sequences

- Initiating activities

- Toddlers are developing more intense interest in the world around them. They ask questions, try things out, and show much more purpose in their play. They can expect things, remember things, and recognize when something is not as it should be.

- Toddlers will bring humor and enthusiasm into their thinking more and more. They will want to show you things and get your help—sometimes.

Toddlers like explanations, but do not change gears easily. If it rains and you were planning on going to the park, they will not always be able to accept the shift in activity. Sometimes they will be very frustrated by any change to a previously stated plan.

Toddlers continue to be very observant and will often imitate what you are doing. They are now trying to take ideas and thoughts and put them together in a series of planned actions. Your toddler is combining experiences and weaving them together, so he may insist on walking around indoors in a pair of boots, carrying a purse and pushing a train around on the floor as he tries to organize his ideas and observations about his world.

Giving Your Toddler Autonomy

- During this period of development, toddlers will be able to decide if they want to build a house or a barn. They can also decide how to do it and carry out a simple plan.

- Toddlers can become more easily frustrated if they can- not execute a plan, so if the big block on the little one keeps falling over, they may need help from you.

- After you show them how to do something, give them space to experiment—they won't always make the cor- rection right away.

Dumping and Pouring Continues

- Toddlers continue to like pouring and dumping. Try providing these opportuni- ties whenever you can.

- Toddlers spill and splash. If you are setting up these types of activities, remem- ber that your toddler will be tempted to pour things on the floor, so you will need to help her remember the rules. Even if you have explained them before, the temptation to spill can override your voice in her head.

- Go into these activities with age-appropriate expecta- tions—this reduces your frustration.

133

MOVING WITH PURPOSE

Once they have mastered walking, toddlers move quickly and with great purpose without seeming to need much rest

Toddlers may be 12, 18, or more than 24 months before they really learn to walk, but when they do, they rarely slow down. They are eager to see the world from an upright position, and they no longer have to think about their movements, as they now have a great deal of muscle memory. By age three, they can run, jump, climb stairs, and even walk backward.

They will begin to combine play and language to express their pleasure or desires. They want to push things, pedal their riding toys, and sometimes climb so high that they cannot come back down.

Toddlers are anxious to see the world, and they keep pushing the boundaries. They still look back to see if you are there,

Physical Milestones

- Walks more smoothly
- Jumps with both feet
- Opens and closes doors
- Balances on one foot
- Pulls up pants with help
- Alternates feet on the steps

Coordination Is Improving

- Toddlers' motor abilities are still rapidly increasing, and so is hand-eye coordination. Their ability to hold a ball and throw it or use a fork and spoon with more ease are all parts of physical development.

- The muscles that control bladder and bowel functions are also developing, which will help when they show interest in toilet training.

but they also expect that you will be there because they want you there. This is part of their magical thinking: I think it is so, therefore it is.

Since toddlers continue to love to climb, it is important to stay close. They often do not see any danger until it is too late. Toddlers are pretty resilient when they do fall, but it is important to spot pieces of equipment or use safety gates at home around stairs or other potentially dangerous areas.

ZOOM

Individual temperament continues to influence how toddlers manage all of their milestones. Some toddlers literally jump before looking, while others watch before they tiptoe in. This means that depending on where your toddler falls on the developmental continuum, you have to help him learn how to understand his own experiences without pressuring him. He will get there in his time.

Seeing Is Wanting

- Toddlers think they can do more physically than they actually can at this age, so they can get frustrated if they see someone doing something like push a scooter and cannot make it work themselves.

- Try talking about their muscles and explain that as they get bigger, their legs will work differently.

Checking Back

- Although they are becoming more and more active, toddlers will continue to need a secure base to explore from, and that base is you.

- Even the most confident toddler needs to see you close and ready to help if need be. When we provide this for our children, we can help them manage their worries as they get farther out in the world.

BIG FEELINGS

Toddlers experience their feelings in much bigger ways as they move past their second birthday

Toddlers grow simultaneously in all areas of development. In cognitive or physical development, toddlers can make huge leaps over short periods of time. With emotional development, it is step-by-step with few shortcuts. Toddlers continue to experience their feelings, but the experience is now influenced by language and their strengthening desire to control the world around them so it feels manageable.

Toddler temperament continues to play an important role. Some toddlers can express their anger or disappointment and move on to another emotional place. Others seem to stay fixed in one spot, unable to let go of whatever they are upset about.

Emotion Coaching

- If you are not comfortable with your own emotions, this may be a good time to read up on the subject or speak with other parents.

- You need to be comfortable with your own emotions before you teach your toddler about his.

- Understanding emotions helps children succeed in school. They learn how to read cues and slow down impulses.

- Working with your toddler helps her develop more trust and greater intimacy with you, which translates to her friendships later on in life.

Ongoing Interactions

- It is easier for us to help children with happier emotions, but we don't choose our feelings, just our reactions and actions. Teaching your toddler to problem-solve will help him throughout his life.

- If the two of you have had a rough time and now are enjoying some good times, point it out. Say, "I am so glad that feelings change. This morning we were angry, but we figured it out together and now we are happy. Good teamwork."

The challenge for parents is to keep our own feelings from escalating. Toddlers often need us to put down breadcrumbs so they can follow a path out of their distress. This may take the form of removing them from a tough situation, even when they are crying or yelling, or offering them an alternative.

Toddler emotions tend to run big, especially sadness, anger, and disappointment. Emotions have a physical sensation, and some toddlers cannot regulate their internal world easily when they are feeling body discomfort. Toddlers cannot pick their emotions, which can leave them feeling vulnerable.

Managing Anger

- Toddlers show much of their emotion when limits are set. They are trying to assert themselves and are not ready to hear that they cannot do something.

- We often have competing needs with our children and need to work to manage our own feelings or impulses. Toddlers' empathy is still in flux, so their ability to understand their feelings in these moments is limited, and they need us to guide them.

Toddler Cries Are Powerful

- Toddlers can be sad, and when we see them cry, we can have different reactions, especially to boys.

- If there was general disapproval of crying where you were raised, it may be hard for you to tolerate your child's tears. See if you can figure out why this is so difficult. Ask yourself what it meant to your parents when you cried, and see if your self-knowledge can guide you through this part of emotion coaching.

HIGH SOCIETY

Social referencing for a toddler is about looking to us for help and understanding

Toddlers need help to understand the world socially. They can go from gregarious and self-confident to shy and uncomfortable in seconds. They are seeing new things, having new experiences, and continuing to broaden the boundaries of their world. They are constantly looking to see what the rules are, and are becoming aware that things change quickly and sometimes without warning. Because they are more aware and can remember how they felt when something happened, they may express resistance to social situations they have loved in the past.

Separation for school or child care may become difficult and painful for toddlers. Those who are socially, emotionally, and

Grandparents' Role

- Grandparents sometimes become primary caregivers for families when parents both work. This can provide your toddler with an opportunity to develop a caring and loving relationship with someone other than her parents.

- No one parents just as you do, and parents are never replaced, no matter how loving the connections are with family. Your toddler will learn what Grandma will let her do and what her parents will let her do and integrate both of these scenarios into her social understanding.

Dads Play an Equal Role

- Fathers play a critical role in the social and emotional development of their children, and the earlier a dad is involved, the better.

- Men and women may have a different perspective on what is fair or reasonable, and children need to understand both perspectives.

- Most importantly, toddlers need to see how their mothers and fathers interact with each other. This is the earliest model of an intimate social system a child has: his family.

cognitively aware that they like school also know it means leaving you, and they do not want that feeling. They may be clingy on playdates or unwilling to venture off to the sandbox or even the next room. Children need to rework their new understandings of the world with each stage of cognitive development.

Your toddler may also decide that going to your friend's house is not what she wants to do. This can be very frustrating. Try giving her time to get used to a plan. Help name her feelings, and stay as steady as you can in the face of tears or anger.

•••••••••••• GREEN ● LIGHT ••••••••••••

Say to your toddler when she is resisting leaving the house, "I know you would rather stay here, but this has to happen now. We will get what we need at the store and then come back home." Remember, toddlers hear what we say even when they do not agree.

Relationships with Other Adults

- Non-family members who care for your toddler can develop meaningful relationships with him. When a caregiver is consistent, safe, and gentle with your toddler, he will learn to trust more people as he ventures farther out from the safety of his home.

- It is always a good idea to drop by unexpectedly to see how well things are going for your toddler when he is left in someone else's care of any sort.

It's Not Fair!

- Sibling relationships are another part of social development for your toddler. She learns about sharing and turn-taking in a very up-close and personal way. Try not to side with one or the other but instead encourage problem-solving.

- When children feel sibling relationships are handled in an unfair way, this can translate to negative peer relationships outside of the house.

TODDLERS SAY A LOT

Language is rapidly becoming the main way toddlers communicate their desires to the world

Toddler language is expanding in leaps and bounds. New vocabulary is increasing daily, especially around things that are meaningful to them. You can explain how the moon can be out in the daytime, and the next day your toddler will search the sky for the moon and tell you why it is there.

Not only is your toddler increasingly able to describe things to you, she now likes to offer explanations of how she understands the world. Toddlers will announce that their grandmother is coming to visit the cat, even though grandma actually lives in another state and is not on her way to your house. These explanations are a combination of experience,

Language Development

- Toddlers continue to learn the names of objects.

- They can combine a few words into simple sentences.

- At 24 months, toddlers have a vocabulary of up to 300 words; by 36 months, this can be up to 1,000 words.

- Toddlers cannot control pitch or volume yet.

- They can use pronouns.

- They start to answer simple questions.

- Toddlers know names for body parts.

- They can relate their experiences to others so you can follow their thoughts.

No Is Powerful

- Toddlers practice saying *no* a lot, but the more you talk to your child, the more she will feel empowered in other ways. Through you, your toddler can learn more language to express her social and emotional development.

- Give your toddler choices, ask her to help, and coach her with words while completing a task with you. By encouraging your toddler to use language, you are helping her work toward greater self-reliance.

actual memories, and the desire to repeat a pleasurable experience all rolled into one.

Toddlers use their explanations of the world to provide comfort to themselves. If it can be explained, it is less unpredictable. From a toddler's perspective, you can make it happen if you express it. Language organizes the world of a toddler. You often hear them explain their world while they play quietly with their toys. If you listen, you may learn what your toddler is trying to figure out or how he experienced something in the past.

Expanding Language

- Toddlers can understand the meaning of language faster than they can express it themselves, so don't be surprised when you ask your partner where the keys are and your toddler goes and finds them.

- Try to help your toddler to expand her language by using words that make connections for her. Say, "If you stand on your toes, you can reach the shelf with the book you want."

Toddlers start to use additional emotional language but still struggle to control their more impulsive feelings. It is difficult for them to say to themselves, "I will be okay if mom says no toy at the store," but you will begin to hear them tell you that they know they cannot get a toy at the store, as though they had resigned themselves to this fact. They are trying to use their understanding of language to slow down their desires, but don't be the least bit surprised when it all falls by the wayside at the toy store.

Playing with Words

- When toddlers listen to older children, they learn more and more about syntax or how different meanings can be. Older toddlers love language play, so use rhymes or songs to change around words and meanings.

- Toddlers begin to recognize that when you hand them the red block and call it green, you are playing around with words.

141

MIRRORING HEALTHY CONFIDENCE

Toddlers show us how they feel about themselves through their assertion of independence and mastery of skills

Toddlers are trying to be both independent and self-assured, though they sense that they do not know how to do everything yet. This is a push/pull time for toddlers and their parents. They want to walk, and then they want to be picked up. They want to get their bucket and go to the park, and then they won't get off your lap once they're there. Toddlers look

to us to see themselves. We are the mirror of their feelings and their successes or failures.

When we ooh and aah at our toddlers, we send a message that they are pretty amazing. A toddler thinks to himself, "Are you talking about me? Why yes, you are!" But then something does not go well—your toddler touches something you have

Avoid Mirroring Shame

- Toddlers continue to see themselves as you see them. If we are mirroring shame in them or mocking them, they cannot separate out or understand this feeling.

- It is important when you cannot control these feelings in you to make yourself a little quieter until the feelings pass. Toddlers do not intend to provoke these feelings. They want to please you, and we need to help them by providing them positive guidance.

Acknowledging Positive Behavior

- When your toddler has done something well, let him know. He needs to hear that you recognize how hard he had worked to do something or how hard it was for him to not grab a toy from his friend when you saw how much he wanted it.

- When your toddler sees that you noticed what he did, you reinforce his problem-solving.

- Praising everything can be as dangerous as praising very little. Try to find a balance.

asked him not to—and you yell. Now your toddler is thinking, "Are you talking about me? Oh no, you are." Toddlers have to combine these reflections and put together all the pieces. This is a lot to take in.

Toddlers integrate their experiences as part of their developing ego and healthy sense of self. They begin to realize that they can please you or frustrate you, and they have to figure out how to please themselves as well.

Building Self-Esteem

- Toddlers need self-esteem to keep putting themselves out in the world. Healthy self-esteem helps children learn to cope with disappointment or difficult times with friends.

- Self-esteem is feeling good about what you know and having the confidence to try new things. Help your toddler understand difficult challenges by listening and explaining and working together.

Asking for Help

- Knowing when you need help and how to ask for it helps build confidence. Start teaching this to your toddler early.

- When she is stuck, ask her if she would like help. And then ask how you can help her.

- Show her you can appreciate help as well. Ask if she can help put the socks in the drawer or carry a bag in for you. Let her know how nice it is to get assistance when your hands are full.

143

SLEEP CHALLENGES

Toddlers who have been sleeping well for months may start to experience sleep interruptions once they turn two

All of us go through times when we do not sleep well, and toddlers are no different. They can now resist going to bed by telling you they want one more book or one more drink and put up a pretty convincing argument. They may react more strongly to daylight saving time changes, start having nightmares, and wake up because they have wet the bed.

Older toddlers are beginning to grow out of daily naps. Try to move up bedtime substantially so your toddler can make up the sleep. If your toddler still needs a nap or gets one at school, try to still stick to an evening routine even if it means your toddler is in his room talking or singing in bed.

Sleep and Daylight Saving Time

- Put your toddler to bed at his normal bedtime.

- Change your clock so it is one hour ahead or behind.

- Wake up and wake your toddler up at the usual time—you will lose or gain an hour of sleep unless you want to adjust your sleep schedule anyway.

- It takes a few days, but he will adjust.

- Your internal clock will be off as well, so get yourself ready for bed earlier than usual.

Giving Up the Crib

- If your toddler crawls out of her crib and you are not ready to move her into a big bed, get a crib tent.

- If you decide to move her into a big bed, start with a mattress on the floor and leave the crib in the room.

- Once she has slept in the bed for a week, begin to talk about the crib going away. Have a good-bye party, and take a picture of her in the crib one last time.

If your toddler has difficulty going to bed, try to start your routine a little earlier. Be predictable and start your transition to bed 10 minutes before your toddler is ready so you have time to go slowly and reassuringly. Let him know you will see him in the morning. When you have finished the last part of your routine, tell your toddler it is time for you to go. If he cries or gets out of bed, tell him he needs to stay in the room. Let him know you will check in after you "wash the dishes," and make sure you go back in after 10 minutes. Repeat as needed, increasing the time between checks.

The first few nights this may be a lot, but don't give up or change your routine. Toddlers look for inconsistencies, and if you change they will persist longer the next night. Continue for a few weeks. Toddlers will soon see the pattern and begin to relax and fall asleep once in bed.

Bedtime Thirst

- Toddlers love to drink before they go to bed, but try to slow down after dinner. If her bedtime is 7:30, give her some water after dinner and remind her that after she brushes her teeth she won't be able to have anything else.

- Especially for toddlers who are working on toilet training, it is important to help them by limiting liquids. If they insist, stick to water.

Bad Dreams

- Nightmares are our way of working out difficult feelings or experiences.

- Toddlers cannot separate reality from fantasy; bad dreams can increase their fears. Remind your toddler that dreams are just pretend. Try to help her relax in her own bed. Sometimes turning her pillow over to the cooler side can help her settle in.

- If the nightmares persist, there might be something going on that is worrying her. Pay attention to her routines to see if something is creating stress.

SAFETY FOR ADVENTUROUS TODDLERS

When you least expect it, your older toddler will discover something that is unsafe

Older toddlers can be misleading. They seem to understand what is safe, and then all of a sudden you see them walking around with a sharp knife that was left too close to the end of the counter. Toddlers still do not realize the potential risks that exist, so we have to stay on our toes.

With the expansion of toddler language, it is important to offer a real explanation rather than just a "no." This helps a toddler hold the experience in memory using higher-level thinking and problem-solving. This is also an age where you can begin to ask your toddler what might happen if she does not strap the buckles of her car seat. Your toddler might say that she will get bumped, allowing you to explain that it is your

Water Safety

- Toddlers cannot discern danger, so their curiosity or impulsiveness puts them at risk. Stay close by to supervise and stay alert.

- Put gates around pools and be sure to dump water out of wading pools.

- Water in toilets or buckets can be just as dangerous, so be sure to safety lock potential drowning places.

- Teach your toddler some swimming safety skills by taking a class together.

- Make sure you know infant/toddler CPR.

Bike Safety Starts Early

- Now is the time to teach your toddler about safety rules for the street and their tricycles and scooters. Even if she does not understand everything, it is important to introduce the language of safety: "This is dangerous because your fingers could get caught."

- Be clear, but don't overdramatize and lose credibility or teach your toddler the world is too scary, even if that is your fear. Use some affect in your tone of voice to emphasize the importance of the message.

job to keep her safe so that won't happen.

It is reassuring for toddlers to hear you say that it is your job to keep them from getting hurt. These interactions can help them when they do not have you near. When we offer information and encourage problem-solving, toddlers will be able to hear your voice in their head, a skill you want to reinforce right through adolescence.

Toddlers are close to the ground, so they are the first to see glass or other sharp objects at the playground. They also are much better at climbing up than down. If your toddler is at the top of a ladder and unsure how to get down, explain what he should do with his feet. It is tempting to reach up and get him, but better to let him problem-solve with your support.

Watching for Risks

- Toddlers can be impulsive, so whenever you are in a new situation, be sure you are aware of potential safety risks.

- If your toddler runs into the road, help her see that unsafe behavior can have consequences.

- Warn your toddler not to do it again, but if she does, help her make connection between her action and behavior. Say, "We need to go inside because you can't play safely out here now. We will try again later."

Taking Care of Themselves at School

- It is important to have safety rehearsal with your children and a plan of action for family safety.

- When your toddler is moving into preschool, ask her to think of ways to stay safe if another child refuses to slide down when they get to the top of the slide. This will help her problem-solve and prepare for situations that are harder to predict.

PREVENTING TOOTH DECAY

Young children are at increased risk for tooth decay without proper dental attention

If you have not taken your toddler to the dentist yet, it is important to get started as soon as possible. Make sure to schedule yearly dental visits. When toddlers have healthy teeth, they can chew more easily and avoid delays in language development. Some dentists will also discuss fluoride treatments for your toddler, depending on your water sources and the dental products you choose. It is also important to eliminate the use of sippy cups and shorten the time children are snacking. Like most things we need to do with children, these are easier said than done, but when you make dental care a goal, it helps you stay on track.

One of the best ways to help your toddler with dental care

Giving Up the Sippy Cup

- Start letting your toddler practice with small amounts of liquid in an open cup.

- When you are ready to transition, let your toddler help pick out new cups.

- Let your toddler help wash the sippy cups and pack them away together.

- Take a deep breath—there will be a few spills and messes until skills are perfected.

Dental Emergencies

- If your toddler has had a fall and hits his tooth hard, take him to the dentist to be sure there is no other serious damage. Baby teeth are pretty hardy, but it is good to check.

- If your toddler has a toothache, rinse his mouth with warm water. If he will let you, apply a cool pack to his face. Sometimes a toddler gets a toothache because something is caught in his teeth—try brushing and flossing.

- Try to prevent dental injuries by safeguarding sharp corners, protruding knobs, or objects that toddlers could fall on.

is by modeling. Try brushing together and work together to find healthy snacks whenever possible. Some parents prefer to take their toddler to a pediatric dentist. If you are dentist-phobic yourself, going to a dentist who specializes in children may help relax you as well. Pediatric dentists have additional training and a good understanding about how children feel when they go to the dentist. They can also recommend some techniques and practices that might help eliminate worries and fears sometimes associated with dental appointments.

Saying Good-bye to Pacifiers

- Pacifiers, bottles, and thumbs: can affect the position of the front teeth. Pacifiers exert force on the front even more than a thumb.

- Talk to your toddler first about what is going to hap-pen. Have a plan, and help her get ready for the day when the pacifier will go in a special box.

- Giving up thumb sucking takes time, and sometimes other lovies can replace the thumb as a soother.

Toddlers and Sugar

- Toddlers, like the rest of us, like sugar. Sugar can speed up dental decay, so try to stick to juices watered down or just plain water when your toddler wants a drink.

- Help your toddler remember toothbrushing and flossing.

HEALTHY CHECKUPS & CHECKLISTS

Well visits can be helpful support sessions for parents and good opportunities to ask questions

Toddlers have a well visit each year. This is a great opportunity to ask questions and get some feedback from your pediatrician. Keep a list of questions so that on the day of your appointment, you can remember all the things you wanted to ask.

Prepare your toddler for this visit in advance. If you have a doctor's kit, you can be the patient and let your toddler give you a checkup. Name the tools in the kit and explain how each is used. Let your toddler hop on and off the scale so he will be prepared for measuring in the office. Doctors often perform a vision and hearing test at the 2- or 3-year visit, so try to walk your toddler through the steps.

Ear Infections

Ear infections can occur a lot in toddlers. Call your doctor if your child shows these signs:

- Pain (most common sign)—more noticeable when toddler is swallowing or sucking

- Loss of appetite, especially if there is pain associated with eating

- Irritability, lethargy

- Trouble sleeping and night waking

- Fever—not all toddlers have higher temperatures

- Ear drainage, sometimes with a color or odor

Managing Health Conditions

- If your toddler has a chronic health condition and she attends school or daycare, make sure you have a health plan on file for them.

- Include a brief medical history, special needs or medication your child may need, precautions to take, and an emergency plan with doctor information. Check this plan twice a year because information can change.

Prepared toddlers usually do pretty well until it is time for a shot. If your child will be receiving immunizations, it is better to let him know a little ahead of time, even if it means sadness and some resistance. Let your toddler know it will hurt a little, but then it will be fine. Sometimes using the words, "That wasn't so bad," when it is done helps a toddler have a little perspective on the procedure. This also will allow you to remind him next time.

Toddlers in day care can get sick more frequently. Try to not be discouraged, because they are building up greater immunity, so when they start kindergarten, they are less likely to get sick. This is also a time to take better care of you. Your toddler usually bounces back in a day or so, while you can struggle with the virus for longer. Take your vitamins, drink water, and try to exercise.

Your Own Health Matters

- Taking care of your own health is important—you are exposed to so many colds, coughs, and flu viruses. New parents can be sick frequently during the first five years as they build up a stronger immune system.

- If you are not feeling well or have extra aches or sore throats, don't wait too long to get medical support for yourself. Taking care of a toddler is exhausting when they are sick and harder if you are not well either.

Each Child Develops Differently

- If you think your toddler has any developmental delays, check with your pediatrician. Developmental milestones are very broad, but sometimes as a parent you can sense when something feels different in your child's development.

- There are many services through Early Intervention programs in your state that are all free for families. This can be a difficult call to make, but a lot of support for families is available.

TRAVELING WITH OLDER TODDLERS

Older toddlers have thoughts, ideas, and language to talk about where they are going now

Traveling with older toddlers definitely has some advantages because they understand so much more. They can help pull their bags, pack up toys and snacks, and talk to you about what is going to happen. When planning a trip, let your toddler know what is coming up. Read books about planes or trains, or talk about driving, so they can begin to prepare

themselves. Set up some chairs in a line and play travel. Present some problems. Say, "Oh, no. This is taking so long." Do some problem-solving together.

When you are on a long car trip, a DVD will only go so far. Bring a basket with active toys to use at a car stop. Include chalk to draw on the sidewalk, ribbons tied on a fly swatter

Preparing for Long Trips

- Make sure you have passports and everything arranged in ample time to avoid last-minute stress.

- Have a brief medical history and updated immunization information with you.

- Keep special medications in your carry-ons and backups in your luggage.

- Bring wrapped presents for your toddler to open along the way. Pick interactive items, like puzzles.

- Consider a layover so you can let your toddler move around and everyone can de-stress.

- If your toddler is restless, try taking an I Spy walk on the plane.

Are We There Yet?

- Long car trips can be difficult. One of you has to do the work while the other parent drives, and this can be exhausting. Try a trip reversal. Leave at your toddler's bedtime, and drive through the night.

- If there is still driving to do, take a break at a hotel during daylight hours. Tag-team with your partner to sleep, and use the pool or hotel facilities to let your toddler play during the day. Resume traveling at nap time or bedtime.

to shake and run around with, or balls to throw. If it is winter, bring a bucket and scoop to shovel snow. If it is raining, bring a large umbrella and boots and splash in some puddles.

After some outside time, many toddlers will be ready for a snack and a nap. Not only will the outside time help them, it will help us with backaches and general travel stress.

···················· GREEN ●LIGHT ··············

When you get back in the car, have a routine. Tell a story with a special travel puppet, have the puppet do some stretching, and take a rest while you play some music. If your toddler is still restless, give him a paper plate and blow some bubbles his way. This will help get out some of the last wiggles before he settles down for a break.

Toddlers Can Enjoy Travel

- Toddlers can now play simple story games in the car or on the plane.

- Take a set of plastic bears or pigs and a box for a house. Play act the story of the three bears or the three little pigs with all the twists and turns your toddler loves. Feed the bears; hide the pigs. Any story can be made travel adaptable this way.

Car Trip Tips

- Bring a ziplock bag with chunky crayons and sticky notes to hang on the window.

- Fill a water bottle with water and oil and drop in some fun little objects such as plastic fish. Seal the bottle top securely, and watch your toddler be curious.

- Tell stories about your toddler into a tape recorder for him to listen to. Add fun surprises like "The day Ethan woke up for school and saw an elephant sitting at the table eating pancakes."

TODDLERS & MEALTIME
Toddlers continue to be in charge of what goes in their mouths

Toddlers will only eat what they want, and coaxing and cajoling only negatively adds to the tone of the mealtime. Toddlers will not starve themselves. It is hard to believe sometimes, but they are not wired that way. They will eat until they are full, and that means something different to them than it does to us. Toddlers have small stomachs, so a few bites go a long way.

If you are worried, keep a log for a week of what your toddler has eaten. This will help calm your worries. If you need to add a vitamin supplement to ensure your toddler is getting what she needs nutritionally, do so. By two, you have a pretty good idea of the colors and textures of food your toddler likes. Continue to offer a variety in small amounts so she can see it, touch it, and taste it. Sometimes it takes more than

Favorite Foods

- Toddlers love pasta. Cook up small batches in different shapes and colors, and serve them with different dipping sauces, such as marinara, guacamole, soy sauce, and cheese sauce.

- They also love chicken nuggets. Here's a great recipe: Mix 1 cup whole-wheat flour; 1/4 teaspoon each salt, pepper, and paprika; 1/4 cup cornmeal; and 1/2 teaspoon oil. Dip chicken pieces into 2 beaten eggs and then into the dry mix. Fry in a wide frying pan in a small amount of vegetable oil, turning when golden.

Preventing Health Problems

- Obesity can be prevented, starting with very young children. Try setting small goals, or you will feel overwhelmed and less likely to keep it up. This takes a different mindset because it is not just what we prepare for toddlers to eat, but what we model eating in front of them.

- Try to creatively increase fruits and vegetables in your family's diet. Have a fresh fruit sundae night where you use yogurt instead of ice cream, and let your toddler scoop his own.

a few days for a child to develop comfort with a new taste. Try to limit choices to only two things at a time. Remember, more choices just support more fussiness on the part of your toddler.

Toddlers continue to do better with smaller meals spread throughout the day. Think of a midmorning snack as an early lunch—another course. That way, you are more likely to give your toddler something nutritious. Toddlers will often want to drink before they eat. If that is the case with your child, make water the beverage of choice. It will help if she is thirsty and won't curb her appetite as much. Try to keep water handy throughout the day.

Temperament continues to play a role here. If your toddler is more resistant to change, how she eats may be impacted. This gets better over time if we allow our toddlers to experiment with new tastes at their own pace.

Packing School Lunches

- Packing school lunches can be hard. You can have him help you once a week by letting him pick foods that are different colors of the rainbow. Toddlers love the idea of eating a rainbow, so use this to increase food awareness.

- Pack small amounts and a wide variety. It is hard to know what your toddler will want the next day. Try small pieces of meat, half an egg, cooked beans, and cheese. Always include something you are sure he will like.

Easy Healthy Snacks

- Homemade biscuits made with a jar of baby-food sweet potatoes

- Hard-boiled eggs cut with an egg slicer for eating ease

- Grated carrots mixed with raisins

- Whole-wheat toast cut into shapes and spread with unsweetened jam or cream cheese

MANNERS

Teaching manners takes time, so start modeling polite behaviors for your toddler early on

When your toddler is sitting in a high chair, you can begin to model appropriate table behavior. Like anything else you say in front of your toddler, he will mimic what he hears. This does not happen quickly, but with patience and humor your toddler will begin to get the hang of things. He will not always understand the meaning, but he will begin to get the intent of the behavior. You can help your toddler beginning with hand washing. Start at least 15 minutes ahead of mealtime so you have plenty of time to play in the soap bubbles. When he is done, have him help you put a spoon and dish on his high chair tray. This will help him make the connection between eating and keeping the utensils on the top of his

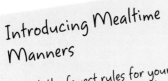

Introducing Mealtime Manners

- Pick the fewest rules for your toddler to follow—less is more. Decide which ones matter the most to you.

- If you model consideration, your toddler will follow along.

- If you want your toddler to stay seated while she eats, try sitting while you eat.

- Toddlers can be overstimulated in restaurants, so try to keep her moving around outside until all the food is at the table.

Cooking Together

- Meal prep is a good way to get toddlers involved.

- Gather a small set of cooking utensils for your toddler to use, and get a colored cutting board for her to work on. Let her choose some of the dishes you will be preparing, but limit choices to two.

- Use engaging words like "blue sky blueberries" or "a puddle of yogurt." All of this enhances the food experience for both of you.

tray. Be as consistent as possible, and try not to use coercion or punitive reactions to do this teaching. Remember that toddlers will tune in more to your tone or affect than the words, so try to be positive.

It can be frustrating for parents when toddlers grab or spit food, so gently remind him to stop. If he continues, you can ignore him, which is often the most effective tool since toddlers tend to stop doing what does not get a response, or you can take him down from the table.

What helps toddlers want to stay at the table more than anything else is when we create a positive and easygoing environment. If you can disengage from how much your toddler is eating and focus more on the together time, the expectations for the meal start to change and eating together can become a positive part of your family rituals.

Practicing Eating Out

- If things fall apart when you visit restaurants with your toddler, try a little dramatic play at home.

- Set up a table in the kitchen and call it Megan's Restaurant. Make menus together. Get out play food and money. Take turns being the family or the waiter.

- Problem-solve some of the things your toddler is struggling with when she goes to a restaurant. Use this play to review behaviors when you are out to eat.

Hands Are Just Faster

- Toddlers will continue to periodically use their hands to eat, so be patient.

- If your toddler is having a hard time managing a utensil, see if she needs a different grip or shape to hold. Some work better than others for toddlers.

- When she eats, sit directly in front of her and model with the same utensil she has, showing the way you hold your hand or turn the spoon. Point out gently some of the ways you are feeding yourself.

FUSSY EATERS

Toddlers by their very nature can and usually do become fussier eaters as they get older

Toddlers become fussier not to make our lives more difficult, but as a part of their desire to become more independent. They cannot distinguish between a good way to show independence to you and a frustrating way until they see, over time, the impact of their behavioral choices.

It can be tempting to use guilt or bribery to get toddlers to eat. Before we know it, we are offering trips to the park or special deserts if only they take two more bites. The only real takeaway children get from bribes is that food is about power—who has it and who wants it. When we become enmeshed in power struggles with our toddlers, we are sending a message that food equals love. It is important to

Preventing Eating Disorders

- Create a healthy eating environment at home.

- Don't skip meals for yourself—model healthy eating behavior.

- Keep your family lifestyle active.

- Have floor time—play everyday with your child.

- Become aware of your own personal attitudes about eating and body image.

- Don't criticize your child's weight.

- Emotion coach.

Fussy Eaters

- Picky eaters may hold fast to their limited diet no matter what you do. Try to keep serving new foods, but do your best to continue to back off from commenting or bribing.

- If your toddler loves muffins, use veggie and fruit recipes to add nutrition value to his diet. If he likes pizza, puree broccoli and mix it into the sauce.

- Be creative, and do the only thing you can do: Buy it, make it, serve it, and wait it out.

avoid confusing the message.

Try to be patient with your toddler. When she is relaxed, she is more likely to try something different. Try to let her help herself, and let her know that she can try another day. Let her see you enjoy the foods you prepare. Most of all, don't spend hours trying to come up with food solutions for your toddler—keep meals simple, small, and easy and continue to introduce new things.

Allow your toddler to choose from the foods you offer, as having a say in what they eat is important to them. It helps them know you listen to them. Let her come to the table and offer again. Wait a few minutes, and give her a chance to see you enjoying your food. If she takes only one bite of something and says she is done, let her get down. She will slowly come around if you stay steady in your resolve. Just like any other developmental task, she will get the hang of it.

Combining Freedom and Food

- Because toddlers love to be independent, get a lunch box and pack it with healthy snacks. Tell your toddler you are putting her special box in the kitchen so if she is hungry, she can get it out herself and bring it to the table to eat whenever she wants.

- You may be surprised what she will eat from her lunch box that she would not touch on her plate.

Fun with Muffin Tins

- Muffin tins make great plates for fussy eaters. Toddlers do not feel as overwhelmed if they see one bite in a 12-pack tin. Ask them to help you fill it with different colors of the rainbow.

- If your toddler finishes one compartment and wants a refill, don't insist he eat something else first. The goal is to have a relaxed meal environment. That will move him faster than any coaxing can do.

FAMILY MEALTIMES
Pick a day, any day, and start the tradition of family dinnertime

Family meals are important for a lot of reasons and can be enjoyed by families of all shapes and sizes. What matters is not the size of your family, but the connections you can make when you are all together.

Life is busy, and sometimes the path of least resistance is to just go with the flow, but the payoff for family dinnertime is huge. At a time when families are under so much stress, these mealtimes can reinforce that parents are there for support. Starting this tradition at an early age helps create important expectations for everyone in the family. Family dinners never have to be complicated. Ordering food in is just as good as making it, and a 15-minute family meal is fine.

The tone of the meal is what is important. Keep it pleasant, fun, and simple. Use this as a time to learn about the day.

Benefits of Family Meals

According to a Harvard study, family meals five times a week have the following benefits:

- Better grades in school
- Better language development
- Better reinforcement of family values
- Less likelihood of substance abuse
- Gives children something to look forward to

Fun with Family Dinners

- Sometimes it is nice to shake things up a bit at family mealtime.

- Purchase a colored plastic tablecloth you can all draw on before you put the food on the table.

- Pick a theme like train dinner and have matching paper plates—a good use for leftover party plates.

- Have a finger food dinner, or use chopsticks to spear things. Toddler brains are novelty seeking, so provide some things for all of you to experience together.

Toddlers can now talk about what they have done and how they felt, and they really like to think about what happened to them during the day. Try not to use this time to complain about your own work schedule or stresses. Even toddlers will pick up on the tension. Focus on the positives, even if you are going through a rough time.

Remind toddlers and older children that sometimes things are hard, but it is so good that even in tough times we all can be together. Turn off phones and televisions. This sends a message to your toddler that all of you matter.

Modeling Thankfulness

- Family meals are a good time to begin teaching thankfulness

- Toddlers don't show appreciation or thankfulness during their first three years, but you can set the stage. Show outward appreciation for what they do.

- At mealtime, go around and say what you like about each other.

- Get your toddler involved in the community. Bring food to a dog shelter, or save pennies to buy mittens for children who do not have any.

Holiday Meal Challenges

- When family is coming, have a dress rehearsal a few days ahead—call it a "pretend holiday." Set out the fancy dishes, use a tablecloth, and talk about where Grandpa will sit and anything else that will be different.

- Since these meals are often longer, have something special for your toddler to do when she is done.

- If manners are more important during this time, have a "please and thank-you party" to practice.

- Keep reminding yourself that if your child melts down, it is not a reflection of your parenting—it is just an emotionally full day.

BIRTHDAYS & ALLERGIES

There are ways to help your toddler enjoy birthday fun, even when allergies limit what he can eat

It can be frustrating and upsetting when your allergic toddler becomes more aware of what he cannot eat at birthday parties. Planning can be challenging because you do not want your child's party to feel different from his friends' parties, but you can deal with the allergies in some simple ways.

If you live in a city that has a kosher parve bakery, you can easily pick up a dairy-free cake, and gluten-free and egg-free cake mixes can be purchased at most high-quality grocery stores. But you can also be creative and avoid serving cake altogether. You can put candles in a Jell-O mold, or in a cup of strawberries or waffles with syrup.

Balancing Diet without Dairy

- Keep toddler protein in the 9- to 34-gram per day range. Beans, tofu, and whole grains have a lot of protein.

- Give your toddler foods high in calcium such as orange juice and cranberry juice.

- Look for foods high in vitamin D such as fortified cereal.

- Add sweet potatoes to toddler diets to get B complex vitamins.

- Offer fatty fishes like salmon as another source of phosphorus.

Coping with Allergy Restrictions

- Toddlers are pretty accepting of allergy limits. They will listen to what you are saying, and even as young as two and a half, will be able to ask someone if their food has dairy or nuts in it.

- When children reach school age, they may express more anxiety and worry, especially if they have severe allergies. If you notice your child is becoming more worried or withdrawn, talk to your pediatrician or go to some of the Web sites that deal with these concerns.

If you want to avoid having cake or ice cream, make some big batches of play dough and give your toddler guests lots of candles and rolling pins to make their own cakes. You can make a banana candle by peeling a banana partway down and putting a cherry on the top when it is time to sing. Since toddlers are not that into food, this becomes a pretty engaging activity.

When your allergic toddler is invited to someone else's party, call ahead and ask the host what the food plans are. Once you know what is planned, you can bring some alternatives for your child and use the party theme to add to the fun. With toddler language developing at rapid speed, you can help your toddler understand why he cannot eat something. When toddlers grow up with this information, they do better managing their reactions.

School and Allergies

- If your child has allergies, make sure your school is food-allergy smart. Provide facts about your child's allergies, what to look for in terms of reactions your child might have, and an emergency plan.

- If your child requires an EpiPen, provide information on how to use one. Make sure anyone who has your toddler for any amount of time has this information.

Frozen Treats

- Finding good recipes is important when you have a child with allergies. Always, regardless of the source, check the ingredients list.

- Here is a great substitute for ice cream that your toddler will love: Freeze bananas that are cut in half, then take them out of their skin. Use a blender or food processor to puree them into a frozen whip consistency.

- Let your toddler top this with fresh fruit, dairy-free chocolate, or even a few gummy bears if this is a special occasion. If your child can have strawberry jam, warm it up a little and let her pour some on like a volcano.

GARDENING WITH TODDLERS

Gardening with toddlers is a way to have a relationship with food that is not as conflicted

Helping children understand and appreciate the connection between gardens and food is not only useful in teaching them about healthy sustainable lifestyles, but it also helps them find pleasure in tasting and trying new foods. Parents do not have much time in today's world to "till the back 40," but we can find some time to bring some of the benefits of gardening into daily routines and plans.

Toddlers are visual learners. Providing hands-on activities that help them see how food and gardens are connected can be a good starting point. If you are not a gardener, you can still introduce a love for growing things. Begin with books that show the connections between nature and what

Food Books for Toddlers

- Yummy Yucky by Leslie Patricelli
- Diary of a Worm by Doreen Cronin
- Fast Food by Saxton Freymann and Joost Elffers
- I Can Eat a Rainbow by Annabel Karmel
- Grandpa's Garden by Sally Kilroy

Easy Gardening Ideas

- Bury some small cucumbers in a plastic container of soil and let your toddler look for surprises in the dirt. Be excited when he finds one. Peel and eat.
- Buy a cherry tomato plant and let him pick off the tomatoes and pop them in his mouth.
- Buy a small watering can and let him water the plants and scoop in the dirt. Look for worms together.
- Tie some apples to a tree, and let him pick one to eat.

is being thrown off the high chair tray. Read *The Carrot Seed* by Ruth Krauss, and buy some big carrots with tops. Let your toddler hold them, wash them, and watch you take a rabbit-like nibble from one. Do this at a non-mealtime. It may surprise you how much more willing your toddler is to try something. Think about all the dirty sand she has popped in her mouth—toddlers can be quite willing to try things that do not seem appealing.

Sharing the Food Experience

- Let your toddler help you pick from a garden or farmers' market. Let her see the process from start to finish. She still may not eat a lot, but she will experience food in a different way.

- Value the process of being together and finding bunches of carrots and picking tomatoes off a plant. This adds to the positive part of the food experience for both of you.

Enjoying Food Preparation

- Many towns and cities have wonderful local markets. Become a regular at the market—walk around with your toddler, and find seasonal things together.

- Try foods out that you have never eaten before. Be curious together, take pictures, and enjoy this non-mealtime food experience.

EXPERIENCES & THE BRAIN

Toddler experiences with play keep the brain developing at a very fast pace

Toddlers learn through play, and as they play their brain shapes and reshapes to take in new information. Brains are wired like electrical circuits, with one thing connecting to another. Information about a toy a toddler is playing with is connecting to the parts of the brain that work with language, problem-solving, movement, emotion, and more. The more a toddler experiences, the more connected his brain wiring will be.

When we encourage our toddlers to problem-solve by thinking, planning, and questioning when they play, they are developing important skills for academic and social success. When you play with your toddler, notice how he reacts to

Older Toddler Play

- Play is more and more imaginative.

- It involves more thinking skills.

- It uses more language.

- Play is more social and expresses feelings.

- It involves more physical skills.

Solving Problems with Play

- Toddlers are now using their play to solve problems and develop logical thinking skills.

- It is hard to imagine how that is happening when a toddler is crashing a truck into another truck, but here is how it works: I want power. Oh, this feels good when I can make things happen.

- Translation: I am experiencing this in my life—a push-pull and a desire to feel in control even when I hear no.

color and sound, texture and light. When falling blocks frustrate your toddler, describe what happened and encourage her to try again. Through play, toddlers learn who they are and how things work. They learn how to communicate, how to use their imaginations, and how to integrate all the things they see and experience in organized themes.

For toddlers, there is no wrong information. They are full of questions and curiosity and are looking for the meaning of things around them. You are their encyclopedia and their guide through their world.

•••••••••••••••• GREEN ● LIGHT ••••••••••••••
When your toddler is playing, give her a chance to do things for herself. She may spill something or struggle, but with your help she will be able to keep trying in a supportive and safe environment. Toddler play is messy, but toddlers make sense of mess when they are hands-on pouring and dumping.

The Power of Dramatic Play

• Helps children learn about and try out different roles: being a mom, dad, or firefighter

• Helps build social concepts and work out problems that occur between peers or siblings

• Increases creativity because it is open-ended

• Allows children an opportunity to safely try out feelings by using their trucks or babies to express their thoughts or feelings

Our Brains Are Different

• Boys' and girls' brains are not identical. Boys are more visual and spatial, and at young ages can mentally rotate an object more easily than a girl.

• Girls are more advanced in putting together visual or language skills and concepts, in part because they operate more out of both hemispheres than boys do.

• This levels out over time, especially when parents help their sons or daughters expand and extend their knowledge without gender bias.

DRAMATIC PLAY

When toddlers reach their second birthday, their play becomes more meaningful and takes on a more organized look

Toddlers begin to do some pretty complex thinking during their second year. They use their play to imitate and invent ideas and challenges. They pretend they are mommies and daddies or that they are actually on a plane. Toddlers can play alone or with your help. They do not include other children in their creative worlds yet because they are trying on all the roles. They use this play to understand gender differences and to safely practice skills before they take them on the road.

Props become important. Toddlers do not need an actual telephone to pretend to talk on one. They will use everything around them and turn it all into a part of their play, as their materials become more symbolic and less concrete.

Themes for Play

• Toddler play can be enhanced in many ways. Add some seasonal items to introduce new concepts and language, such as picnic baskets and flags in July, or a small bucket of little pumpkins in October.

• In January, collect your single mittens and fill them with little animals, then read a story about the lost mitten. All of these ideas increase calendar awareness and changes in times of the year, and you can find everything you need easily.

Ice Cream Store Props

• Put together an ice-cream store prop box. Use extra ice-cream scoops and big pompoms for ice cream. Save a few old ice-cream containers to add to the effect, and get some extra props from your local ice-cream shop. Add some play money, and you are good to go for a rainy day.

• This is a great activity if you have some tasks of your own to complete. Put this away after a few days so it maintains some novelty.

When you play with your toddler now, take the backseat. When you take a secondary role, your toddler can experience being the leader and making decisions. Repeat and reflect back what she is saying to you so she can hear her internal voice and react to it. This kind of play allows toddlers to practice taking turns. When toddlers are with peers, changing roles is still too complicated, and play rules are still being sorted out.

······· GREEN ● LIGHT ·········

Toddlers love boxes as props. Get a long wardrobe box, and climb in with your child to hibernate. Bring in books and a flashlight. Growl and be silly. With a little help, a toddler can turn this box into a cave for a family of bears, a fire station for trucks, and so much more.

Imaginative Play

- Puppets and stuffed animals often take on a greater role in imaginative play if you bring them in as an enhanced prop.

- If you are planning a trip to the zoo, gather all the different wild animals your toddler has and make a zoo in your living room. You can talk about what you are going to see when you get there, and when you return your toddler will bring more information to his play.

Gender Awareness

- Boys and girls will start to be more gender aware in their play at around 30 months. By three or four, they can identify themselves as a boy or girl and also understand who else is a boy or girl and that you grow into a man or woman. Culture, both at large and your own family expectations, play a significant role. This is a good time to talk with your partner about how stereotypes affected each of you growing up.

FLEXIBLE TOYS
Older toddler toys should be interchangeable, as children move from concrete to symbolic play

Toys become stage props for toddlers at this age. Toddlers combine materials and use parts from one toy to put in another. They are much more intentional with their play now, so they often look for real-life objects for play. This is probably one of the least expensive times for purchasing toys because toddlers are not in tune with cultural pressures for things.

They are extremely happy with boxes to crawl into, old cell phones to talk on, keyboards, and fly swatters (clean ones) to drag around the house. These things are the real deal and lend themselves perfectly to what toddlers are pretending to be, which is you.

Blocks are probably the most long-lasting and important

Toys for Older Toddlers

- Blocks—different kinds, shapes, and sizes

- Puzzles

- Manipulative or connecting toys that hook together

- Props for playing house, fire station, or any other pretend world your child likes

- Small people that can fit in and out of trucks or block buildings

Recycling Toys

- Recycling toys can be important for space, but it can be difficult for toddlers to let go even if they have not played with a toy for a while.

- Try to go through your toddler's toys every few months. Throw out broken pieces, but also look for new ways to combine incomplete sets. A puzzle with food pieces can now be used in the housekeeping corner.

purchase you can make. Cardboard blocks are inexpensive and can be put together in so many ways. They are sturdy enough for toddlers to walk on, and are tall enough for toddlers to hide behind them. The boxes take an hour or two to assemble, but once you show your toddler what they can do, they will quickly become a favorite.

Playing with Wagons

- Toddlers love to pull, so a wagon to move around can be a very flexible toy. You can go rock or leaf collecting.

- If you have construction going on near your house, let your toddler fill up his wagon with construction vehicles and go down to visit the work site. Taking these pieces to visit the real deal can enhance play.

Make It Yourself

- Homemade play dough takes more time, but it can be a great activity. It is fun to make and is initially warm, which changes the experience for your toddler. You also get a bigger mound, which looks different and encourages a different kind of play.

- Salt trays are another quickie. Pour table salt on a cookie sheet and add little cars and trucks and little spoons for scooping. Use at the kitchen table together.

171

BOOKS & MORE

When we read to toddlers, we are preparing them for learning how to read themselves

Reading provides toddlers with many valuable gifts. Perhaps the most important is the close nature of the interaction, snuggling up in bed or on the couch together. Books give toddlers exposure to worlds they may not see otherwise and provide language opportunities through sound and tone.

Reading should be fun, but for many toddlers sitting still is a challenge. If your toddler is too busy to sit, try making a cave with blankets and reading inside or bringing along a related book when you go out on an excursion. This can trigger interest in the book later on.

When you read, have a good time with your toddler. Before

Setting up Reading Spaces

- Have book spaces in several rooms.

- Cushions or pillows help create a nest feeling.

- Soft lighting can help create some quiet, calming times—great use for old nursery lamps.

- Find some small baskets to keep books in, and change titles every month.

- Hang pictures—the library often gives away book jackets, which make great wall hangings.

Books for Different Seasons

- Highlight seasonal books to help prepare your toddler for changes in weather. Libraries are great resources for these kinds of books.

- Try reading a cold-weather book on a blanket outside on a snowy hill, or take out a flashlight and read a night-time book on your porch or patio in the summer. Take out your toddler's bath books and read a book while you sit under an umbrella in the rain.

you turn the page of a favorite book, ask him what he thinks is coming next. Be delighted with him when he sees that it was exactly what he thought. Point to pictures, and ask questions. Be creative yourself. Wonder aloud if the dog in the picture is going to find his bone or get into trouble. Toddlers love to wonder with you, and you can add some of what is specific to your toddler into the books you read.

You can also begin to point out that there are words all around us. Read the cereal box or the sign at the park. Toddlers will begin to make the connection that those marks we call letters are everywhere. This is a great age to go to the library and take out books. Toddlers love the notion of borrowing and returning books. You can begin to experiment with different types of books to see if your toddler is ready for those with more details or storyline. If you speak another language at home, you can also find books to represent aspects of your cultural diversity.

Favorite Reads

- With your help, toddlers will find authors who they really like. Colors and drawings can really pull a toddler's interest in.

- Check parenting Web sites for new good reads, or visit your favorite authors' Web sites for new books. Experiment with different categories of books, but keep the oldies but goodies close by.

Learning the Written Word

- Reading, writing, and drawing are all parts of your toddler's learning about the written word.

- Let your toddler make a book—just staple some pages together and let her draw away. When she is done, ask her what the book is about. Name what she is doing: You are writing a book, and that is what authors do.

HOW TO PLAY

Play may become harder for parents as toddlers get older and play becomes more complex

Toddlers love dramatic play, and for many parents this world seems daunting. But children will guide us all the way. Toddlers do not think in linear ways, so when they play they pull in thoughts and ideas from everything they see and hear. If we try to correct or lead them, they can become frustrated or disengaged.

Here are a few things to try when you are playing: Begin by limiting it to 20 minutes of real play time a day, when you are focused and not distracted. Once you get the hang of it, increase the time as much as you want. Make sure you are comfortable, have gone to the bathroom, had a snack, and are sitting where it is easiest for your body. If it is on the floor,

Observing Your Toddler Play

- Observing your toddler play gives you good information. It helps you know how he uses his voice and body during play.

- Toddler play provides insight into how she

problem-solves with her toys or props and lets you know best how to guide her when she is stuck. This also allows you to step back and see where sometimes the two of you may get into power struggles.

Connecting throughout the Day

- You can have connected time with your child at play and at naptime. Sing or whisper together, or talk about what she might like to dream about.

- Toddlers at this age have things to say, so try to be a good listener. Add things but let them lead. When it is time to move on, let her know how much you liked this time together.

try a pillow. Start playing side-by-side with your toddler. Stir something or run a car up a ramp. Your toddler will approach very quickly to see what is up. When she does, she will probably take whatever you have or give you something to add to the mix. Take it, or give up what you have, and let her begin leading.

When your toddler tells you something, mirror her. For example:

Toddler: "I want my baby doll."

Parent: "Oh, you want the baby now?"

Toddler: "Yes, it is my baby."

Parent: "Yes, you are right. It is your baby. I was holding it. Does your baby need anything?"

Toddler: "She needs a bottle."

Parent: "Oh, yes, she needs a bottle. She is probably hungry."

Your toddler will keep going. With just a little reflection and some connecting information from you, she will help you play. We do not need great ideas: Our toddlers have those—we just need to follow.

Adults Play Differently

- Watch your partner play sometimes. You each bring different ideas into play, and if you stay open, you can integrate some new techniques.

- Try not to interfere with play when your toddler is really engaged with another child or adult. Watch and see what she does and how she is thinking and feeling.

Play as a Window

- As your toddler plays, you will see where he needs more information. If he is having a hard time expressing himself, introduce some books that focus on feelings or bodies, especially after something significant has happened in his life.

- Play is the window to how your toddler is thinking about the world. Toddlers need information and opportunities to understand new experiences. They need to practice to gain mastery.

ART, MUSIC & DANCE
Creative arts are the glues that help toddlers develop logic and problem-solving skills

Children are natural-born artists. They can tell stories, paint freely, and move their bodies around without embarrassment. To keep this intact for them as they get older and more self-conscious, it is important to make these areas of learning as much a part of their play as the toys they use now or the computers they will use later on.

Classes can help support the arts, but the real learning is done through open play and experimentation. Playing music during the day is important for children, not just as background but to really move or think to. Give toddlers some ribbons, put on some classical tunes, and let them glide, or try a little reggae. Watch how they change the way they move

Encouraging Creativity

- Creativity helps bridge knowledge for each of us in a way that is uniquely ours. This opportunity to self-express can help toddlers continue on a path that supports emotional health as well as physical health and well-being.

- When you provide your toddler with a drawing tablet, she can hold a crayon or marker and feel the movement in her body. She can observe color and texture and see herself acquire more skill with materials.

Drawing Starts by Scribbling

- Toddler drawings may look like scribbles in the beginning, but your child is learning how to have more and more control and choice over what she does.

- Somewhere during her second year she will be able to draw more lines and pat-

terns that are recognizable to her and to you. Ask her what she is drawing, and don't get tempted to add a face to her work. She will become more and more creative with opportunity and non-critical support from you.

176

their bodies. Put musical instruments out for them, such as bells with handles, autoharps, or a tambourine. You do not have to know how to play an instrument to use these. They sound great, and your toddler and you can play together.

Sing with your toddler. It is a different way for him to practice using his voice, and singing comes from a different part of the brain, so it enhances language development. If you are not sure what to sing, sing what you like. You can always take a familiar tune and add words like, "We are going to the park."

Art is wonderful but it can be very messy, and it should be. Spread a plastic sheet down on the floor to paint. Strip your toddler down, and put an old T-shirt of yours on him, which will have much more coverage and be easier to clean up afterward. Beginning paint can just be water and food coloring, which is less messy and still lets toddlers practice with color and brushes.

Feel the Beat

- When toddlers paint or draw, listen to music, or dance, they are developing emerging reading skills. There is a beginning and end in reading, and how to stop and start your body when you dance is part of that learning.

- Music has beat and rhythm, and so do the words on the page. All of these experiences are connecting the wiring for later academic skills.

Try a Concert

- Take your toddler to a park to hear music, or stop to listen to street musicians. Let him see live performances as well as listen to the radio, iPod, or CDs.

- If you play an instrument, let him play with you, but if you don't play, keep providing opportunities for him to experiment with sound.

- Avoid showing him how to do it at first, as this can dampen his innate curiosity. Wait until he asks you to help him learn something.

FRIENDS & FAMILY

As toddlers get older, their awareness of who is important to them becomes more defined

As toddlers get older, they become aware of who matters in their world, and they begin to express it with both language and actions. They may now run to their grandmother's arms or climb up on their teacher's lap. Toddlers between 24 and 36 months are able to take what they have learned from the safety of their relationship with you and transfer some of that information to other grownups in their lives.

Having family around can be wonderful for children, but it is not always possible. If your families are not close by, there are many ways to help your toddler feel connected to them. When you visit, take videos to show your child later. Tell her

Siblings Have Lifetime Relationships

- Siblings have unique relationships as both family and friend. Toddlers develop appropriate interactions with their siblings over time.

- Much of what your toddler will model will be how he sees you problem-solve the challenges of having more than one child. Toddlers will learn about waiting for turns, sharing your time and attention, feeling protected, and feeling vulnerable. These are the same ingredients that make up the challenges of friendships with his peers.

Toddlers on the Watch

- When you observe your toddler at a family event, you can see where both her comfort in a group lies and also where her challenges are.

- She may be fine with other adults but shy away from her cousins. She may not get off your lap, or disappear with the others, or both. She is watching—observing not only children but how safe all the grownups make the environment emotionally and socially.

stories about your parents' house, describing the things she might see when she goes. Keep photo albums around for her to look at.

Remind your toddler what he did when his grandparents came to visit and how nice it will be to see them again. If your family members are more hands-off when they visit, remind your toddler about how Grandpa liked to watch him play while he read the paper. This helps toddlers create a story in their own minds about the meaning of these visits and the special people in their lives.

ZOOM

As your toddler creates attachments to other adults, you will see that his ability to navigate separation becomes more sophisticated. He will be able to use his existing emotional connections to create a different level of social connection now. If you have regular playdates with friends, you will see your toddler become increasingly able to be comforted or helped by another mom.

Families Weigh In

- Friends and family can be well-meaning but also very critical when they observe children clinging or being overly active or impulsive. Parents can feel anxious wondering how their toddlers will behave.

- Try to remind yourself that what people see about your toddler in a group setting is only a very small part of what makes up her personality. Once you put it in perspective, it is easier to emotion coach and help your toddler when she is stuck.

Friendships Matter

- Friends are important in life—they keep us from feeling isolated or alone. They can support us and comfort us when we are in pain or afraid, and help us keep bigger perspectives on the world.

- Take time to think about why friendships are important to you and what makes a good friendship. This will help you set the guiding principles for your toddler.

TOO MUCH STIMULATION

Toddlers are not always able to tell you they have had too much activity

Toddlers need to have stimulation to be challenged, but trying to find a balance for your child is important. This is where understanding your toddler's temperament can be helpful.

If your toddler takes time to warm up, he may need help getting started with an activity but will be fine once he gets going. Some toddlers jump in and join right away, but

struggle to disengage until they are falling apart. How you understand your toddler's style of activity helps guide your decision-making about how many activities you need to plan and how stimulating these activities should be.

Toddlers don't need to have classes to get enough stimulation, but many parents enjoy the social connections they

Taking a Break

- Toddlers take in enormous amounts of information without a very good mechanism to shut it off or slow it down.

- Pay attention to the clock. When your toddler has been running around outside for an hour, provide a break. This models ways

she can do better self-care when she is away from groups.

- During the next year she will become better able to ask for what she wants before she melts down, but for now it is still important for you to make it part of the routine.

Opening New Worlds

- As toddler brains continue to be novelty seeking, trips to museums—especially ones geared to children— can be wonderful. Try to go early in the day when noise and activity is generally less.

- Try not to make your first trip together to a museum a time when there is a special exhibit where there might be a lot of extra stimulation.

- Take pictures when you go with your toddler so you can make a book for her to look at later.

make at them, and that is a good enough reason for you to sign up for one if you can. Parenting can be isolating, and having something to look forward to can help us parent more effectively. When choosing a class, try to match it to your child's needs: If she is a lap sitter, you may want a slowly paced gym class to get her comfortable moving. If she loves getting messy, an art class that provides an opportunity to do so may work better.

Whatever activities you choose, formal or informal, you will see that your toddler needs help at times if he becomes overstimulated. Toddlers do not always have or use the words to tell you they need help, but their body language is usually spot on. They may turn away from activities, look distracted, pull out of the main group of children, or become more frenetic in their play, pushing or knocking others over. These behaviors can happen 10 minutes or 45 minutes into a planned activity.

Taking Time to Relax

- Relaxing on the go can be difficult, but important. Talk to your toddler a little ahead of time about the day. Let him know that there will be busy times and time to relax.

- You may only last an hour. If he has been fussy and you decide to leave, say, "We will try another time to stay longer. I can see that it feels too busy inside for you right now."

Slowing Down

- Helping your toddler unwind when you are out can sometimes be done more easily if you plan the breaks and let her know ahead of time what the general routine will be.

- If you are visiting the zoo, let her know that after you see the monkeys it will be time to find a quiet spot to relax and read the monkey book and have a snack. This helps your toddler learn how to pace herself.

PREPARING FOR SCHOOL
Toddlers need your help transitioning to preschool or day care

Children often start preschool programs, full- or part-time, during their toddler years. Helping your toddler with the adjustment is an important part of their daily routine. Once you have selected a program you like, plan some visits with your toddler. Don't plan on leaving the school the first few times, so your toddler can comfortably explore the environment. Your child not only will be sizing up the physical and emotional environment, but also paying attention to how other toddlers are comforted when parents leave and whether the teacher's expectations are manageable.

There are two tasks toddlers need to manage in this situation: being away from you, and learning what happens at school. These two tasks usually occur consecutively, so try not to be discouraged if your toddler is still trying to get

Helping Your Toddler at School

- Talk to your toddler about what he wants to play with when you leave—this will help him plan ahead.

- If your toddler does better being handed to a teacher, work it out ahead of time so the teacher is prepared for the handoff.

- Make sure you say good-bye when you are ready to go.

- Remind your toddler that you will be back.

- If he is sad or upset, name the feeling.

- School transitions take different amounts of time for different toddlers. Remind yourself as much as you need to that it will get better in time.

A Life of Her Own

- When your toddler has made a transition to school and the separation from you seems easier, she will have experiences that you won't be directly involved in. You will be relying on teachers' notes or conversations to piece together what has happened.

- Ask toddlers specific questions. Say, "Did you paint today? Did you use the red or yellow paint?" More open-ended questions about their day are much too difficult to answer.

comfortable after a couple of weeks. It may take up to six weeks for her to feel as though she understands not only the transition from home to school, but also the school routines.

Try to leave plenty of time in the mornings for your toddler to get ready. Most toddlers like to play when they wake up and will not do well if they are rushed. If you do not have a lot of time, try cutting short some of your other morning routines, such as breakfast, so your toddler can use that time to do her own thing at home. Bring dry cereal and fruit for her to eat on the way so you can maximize home time. Most schools offer a morning snack or will allow your toddler to eat something once she gets to school.

Different Behaviors, Different Places

- Toddlers learn new routines and have new expectations. They may clean up or put on their own shoes. Children are interested in what their peers are doing and are often willing to experiment if they see their friends try something.

- Toddlers also miss school routines when they are away. They miss seeing friends and being part of the activities. It may take a day or two when you are on vacation to get used to the lack of routine. It may also take them a couple days to get acclimated when they return.

The World Is Diverse

- When selecting a program for your toddler, either full- or part-time, try to see how the staff work with families. Are they open to different cultural values and beliefs? How do they handle situations where children may speak a different language?

- Knowing how the school organizes staffing and helps meet family needs is important when you are trying to help your child feel comfortable in a new setting.

183

GROUPS OF TODDLERS

When you see a group of toddlers in a room, you are observing every emotion you can imagine

Toddlers and groups don't always go well together. In some ways they thrive on the energy of a group, and in other ways they retreat from the intensity. Helping your child with his feelings is the most important part of toddler grouping.

Toddlers in child care are not only playing around other children, but also being cared for, fed, dressed, changed, and napped in the presence of others all the time, so they are essentially living part-time with other toddlers. They need to know that their needs matter, so when you select a child-care setting for your toddler, the skill of the caregiver will be the most important ingredient.

We know toddlers can and do cry, scream, resist, hit, bite,

KNACK RAISING YOUR TODDLER

Finding a Match

- Age-appropriate groups can vary depending on your toddler.

- If she is pretty verbal, it may be helpful to be in a group of children with a slightly broader age range so she can engage with peers through speech. This

is not a one-size-fits-all. If the program lets you choose, observe her in both settings.

- What matters most is that the staff knows how to understand developmental differences and plans around this knowledge.

Connecting with Other Parents

- When our children are in child care or shorter programs away from us, we may not get to meet many of the other parents. It can be helpful for your toddler to see you connected to the school setting in some adult ways.

- Try to greet other parents when you walk in, and learn some of their names. Your toddler is paying attention to how you feel about the space and the community that is there and will imitate what he sees.

and push when they are frustrated or sad. What we can look for in any setting is a staff that can see this behavior for what it is—normal. Normal does not mean that we have to like or accept it, but it does mean that teachers must help children understand their feelings and find better, more helpful ways to deal with them.

Children will often respond to shaming, guilt, or fear, but what these adult behaviors do not model is a way to cope with feelings of anger or worry in a healthy, positive way. When toddlers get help with their emotions early on, they develop empathy for others and increased problem-solving skills. This takes time and trust between a toddler and his caregiver. When they get their needs met—physically, emotionally, and socially—toddlers can learn to accept limits and routines in a calmer and safer way, which helps them repeat their own experiences with their toddler friends.

Doing the Best We Can

- All parents experience times when they feel they are being judged. Many parents try to say they do not care, but it impacts us even if it is subtle.

- Often in these situations we feel that our toddler is different, not complying. Tell yourself over and over again that this is why you are bringing your toddler to a group—to learn how to slow down and practice social skills. Your toddler is doing the best he can in the moment.

Art Groups and More

- Classes can be really fun for toddlers now. Let your toddler have some choices over what he would like. You may want him to take a music class, but he really wants to go to a messy hands-on art class.

- Let your toddler explore his interests. They will change over time if you allow him to have some control when he can.

SEPARATION ANXIETY
Toddlers can have a recurrence of separation anxiety or still be working on their earlier skills

From a very early age, children perceive differences in the relationships they experience. Toddlers begin to recognize that in addition to mom and dad there are other grownups that seem to respond to them in positive and affectionate ways. Toddlers, no matter how close a relationship they develop with babysitters, nannies, or family members, are not confused about who their primary caregivers are: you. Even so, there will be times they jump into someone else's arms or refuse at first to jump back into yours.

Toddlers are working on learning how to manage their emotions. If they linger in someone else's arms, they are feeling glad you are back but also not sure if you are going to stay. They will

Toddler Separation Tips

- Give your toddler something of yours to hold: a handkerchief or a stuffed animal you kiss and leave in his arms.

- Teach him the emotional language: "You have a feeling called 'missing' right now."

- Practice separating with gradually increased lengths of time.

- Have the sitter or your partner leave at the same time you do to go for a walk.

- Help your toddler engage in an activity if she is sad or upset.

- Give her some time to cope with the feelings. Missing is not easy.

Separation Anxiety

- Separation anxiety is normal and can occur between seven months and three years of age.

- For some children, life stressors such as a new baby or a move can trigger it. Emotion coaching is very important. Identify feelings, and follow through with whatever your plan is. It will pass.

- Some toddlers may also prefer one parent over another during these times. It is important not to take it personally.

be cautious as they process that you have returned and allow themselves to feel relaxed again with mom or dad. These can be uncomfortable or painful moments for us as parents, and we need to be careful that we interpret these exchanges for what they are: your toddler learning how to transition and organize his emotional thoughts, not punishment for your having left.

As toddlers get older and develop more language around separating, they will begin to tell you directly why they need help coming or going, but until then you have to do that work with them.

When Good-Byes Go Badly

• Separating from your toddler can go badly for many reasons. Some children are more sensitive to changing routines and have a harder time regulating their feelings. If you know this about your child, practice before she starts a program. This might mean building extra time into your schedule.

• Go away for 10 minutes and then come back for 30 minutes. Repeat. Be matter-of-fact when you return. Call it a day, and try again for the next few days. She will get the hang of it.

Our Own Ambivalence

• Sometimes separating from your toddler becomes difficult because you are unclear about what feels good for you. Sometimes it can feel gratifying to see our toddlers only want us.

• If you find yourself aware that you are sending a mixed message, take some time to reflect on what your goals are before you continue with the separating process. It will make it easier on your toddler when you are clear with yourself.

BRINGING A NEW BABY HOME

The introduction of a new sibling is an exciting and unpredictable moment

Toddlers respond in many different ways the first time they see you with their new baby brother or sister. Sometimes this introduction takes place in the hospital, and sometimes at home. If you are bringing your toddler to the hospital, remember that he will be on high alert. He will have spent some time away from you with just dad or grandparents,

coming to a new place that is very large and often smells funny. He will have a sense that this is somehow important but not really know what that means.

Give him the space to explore. Have some things for him to do when he comes. Let him check out the baby slowly. Some toddlers will go to their mother's arms right away, and some

Coming Home

- Your toddler may be very ready to hold the new baby, but try to let him decide when and for how long. Ask him what he sees when he looks at the baby.

- Try to not to overreact the first time you see the two

of them together. Be calm, and let him know what will happen next. Say, "When you are done holding the baby, will it be time to play or go to the park?" Keep to routines as much as possible.

Home from the Hospital

- Toddlers may fall apart the first day or two you are home from the hospital. They may be tired, and often there is company or family bringing food or visiting.

- If you can hold off outside guests for a day or two, it can help. Sometimes your toddler will just not be happy with anyone but you. If your partner is there, let him hold the baby while you have uninterrupted time with your toddler.

will stay back a little. This is their uncertainty showing. They are not angry with you, though that may be your fear—they are just unsure.

If you are introducing your toddler to the baby at home, see if someone can take your toddler out for a while so you can settle into the house before she comes in. When she comes in, let her come to you as quickly or slowly as she needs to, and then you can ask if she would like to see the baby. Try to avoid asking how she feels because she will not yet know.

You can remind your toddler of all the ways you got ready for the baby before he was here. Let her look at or touch the baby's feet and tummy. If she wants to hold the baby, get her comfortable on pillows on the floor and place the baby in her arms. Point out how wobbly a baby's body is and explain we have to use our muscles to hold a baby. When she is done holding the baby, let her stay close.

Toddlers show various amounts of interest in new babies. Any reaction is normal and not a predictor of good or bad things to come. Toddlers need to live the experience before they will understand how this has impacted their lives.

Family Time

- Toddlers, older children, and even babies can and do compete for your attention. When there is discord, try not to assign blame to anyone. Keep it neutral. Say, "I can see you both want a lot of help from me right now."

- Older toddlers can engage in some problem-solving, so ask them what they think would be a good solution. If they come up with an impossible one, explain why. Keep it simple, and ask what else might work.

Jealousy, Not an Easy Emotion

- If you think your toddler is experiencing jealousy and having a hard time, make sure you name the feeling.

- Help your toddler problem-solve. Say, "What do you think will help you with that feeling?"

- Be matter-of-fact if she tells you to throw the baby out. Let her know that would not be safe and that your job is to make things safe for both of them.

- Be empathic. Try saying, "It is so hard to wait for me to be done."

- Try not to blame your toddler. She has no experience with this either.

189

TODDLER FRIENDSHIPS WITH PEERS
Older toddlers are becoming more and more attracted to the play of others

Some toddlers will want to join in, while others will want to watch others play and try out what they saw when they are at home, feeling safe. When you are with your toddler playing at the park or at a friend's house, you need to stay close and be ready to help if needed. Sometimes help takes the form of active participation, and sometimes it means just staying close and seeing if our toddlers can problem-solve themselves.

Trying to decide whether to jump in and settle a conflict or hang back a bit is complicated because you never know what another parent might say or do. Sometimes it helps to say to another parent, "Would you be okay for a minute if we

KNACK RAISING YOUR TODDLER

Increasing Friendships

- Talk to your toddler about your friends. If you are angry or frustrated with a friend and your toddler is nearby, talk to her about what she might have heard. Say, "I was trying to work out a problem with my friend. Sometimes it is hard to do."

- Toddlers pay attention, so do your best when they are around not to talk about others in a demeaning or blaming way. They will model and imitate much of what they hear.

Bully Behavior

- There are many contributing factors to bully behavior, so it is important to make it a high priority to help expand your toddler's problem-solving skills, empathy, and emotional understanding.

- If toddlers are frequently exposed to adult bullying, they will be at greater risk to repeat the behavior. Assess environmental influences for yourself and your family so you can minimize these exposures.

watch and see how they handle it?" If the toddlers can figure out a good enough way to share something (even if it does not look good enough to us), try to let it be. You can say to the two toddlers afterward, "It looks like you found a way to take turns."

When toddlers are playing, we can provide them with emotional language as needed: "I can see that Justin is crying because he wants his shovel back." This does not mean your child will give Justin his shovel back, but you are beginning to help him understand someone else's feelings, and this is

part of developing empathy. You can try offering suggestions and remind your toddler about how he felt when he did not have one of his toys. Over time, toddlers begin to work these understandings into their social play.

Dealing with Conflict

- It is important to help your toddler learn how to work with conflict. Conflicts within friendships are part of life.

- When you see your toddler engaged in a conflict with a peer and they are upset, go over to them. Treat them both with understanding. Say, "Looks like you are both angry and want the same toy. It is not okay to hit friends. What else can we do? I will help you find a better idea."

Toddler Friendships

- Friendships are important to older toddlers. They have begun to see themselves as part of the world while finding pleasure in connections and sadness when things fall apart.

- Things can go so well and then fall apart abruptly. If your toddler has had a rough day with friends, it can be helpful to have a picture album of his friends. Talk to him as you look at the photos. Try to help him with his feelings.

POTTY TRAINING READINESS

Toilet training takes time, so being ready is important for you as well as your toddler

Knowing when your toddler is ready to use the toilet is important. Toddlers need to be able to control their bodies—their bladders and bowels— before they can use the toilet. Try to relax if your child is not showing any emotional interest. Many children are not out of diapers until three and a half years of age.

When your toddler is ready or getting ready, you will notice that she is able to stay dry for a couple of hours. Naptime dryness is one indicator of this. Toddlers will also begin to tell you they are peeing, especially when they are ready for a bath or change. You can give your toddler some language, such as, "I am glad you noticed what your body was doing."

Can I Come In?

- Toddlers become fascinated by what happens when you go to the bathroom. If you are comfortable, let them come in to play.

- If they are watching you, comment on what you are doing. Say, "I am peeing now. I don't wear a diaper, so this is where I have to put my pee." Be matter-of-fact with your explanation.

Toilet Readiness

Toddler readiness can be anywhere between two and four years of age. Here are some signs:

- Going dry for at least two hours

- Showing increased interest in the toilet: asking to sit, hand you paper, or flush

- Becoming increasingly uncomfortable in their diapers

- Finding private places to void or move their bowels

This cues her that paying attention to her body seems to interest both of you.

Toddlers also need to be able to do some self-help to be successful when they potty train. You can begin to help them pull up their own pants. The ability to follow simple instructions makes it easier for them to follow the steps necessary for using the toilet when it is time.

It is important that you pick a time to potty train your toddler when you do not feel pressured or rushed. Helping a toddler learn to use the toilet takes time and can be messy or inconvenient. Try to avoid potty training before a big change, like a new baby or starting preschool. If you begin to feel that your toddler is reacting to the stress, no matter how ready she might have been, take a step back, breathe, and wait another week or two. You will both do better.

Toilet Paper Everywhere

- Your toddlers may be fascinated by toilet paper but not quite ready to do the work. Ask her if she would like to try sitting, but accept her answer.

- Pressure on her early in the process can lead very quickly to increased resistance. If she does not want to sit, let her throw some paper in and flush; this is a beginning.

Make Hand Washing Fun

- Hand washing is an important part of bathroom use, so when you go to the bathroom, invite your toddler to wash her hands.

- Talk about scrubbing both sides and how good it feels. Use some nice soap or get a fun dispenser and let her smell the scent. Find a hand-washing song to sing to encourage a few more seconds in the process.

PARENTS' ROLE IN POTTY TRAINING

Knowing what you are responsible for in potty training makes the job easier

You cannot, as much as you try, make your child ready to use the toilet. If you do your work, your child will be ready at some point to do his job. Each day to a toddler is a whole new experience. Because he wanted to use the toilet Monday does not mean he wants to do it Tuesday, so let him decide each time what he is going to do.

Teach your toddler about his or her body. Use easy language. Try to use accurate words to talk about body parts. You do not have to get too detailed, but you are going to want to say, "Your pee [or urine] just came out. Here is some toilet paper to wipe your bottom [or vagina]." Find your comfort level with language.

Toddler toilet responsibilities are few, but critical to respect:

- Deciding whether she is going to use her diaper or the toilet.

- Learning her own body signals—fullness or discomfort and so on.

- Going at her own pace.

- Remember these really are your toddler's to decide so focus on what your own role is with toilet training.

What Should We Call It?

- Once your toddler is engaged in some level of practice, try to have some body books around so you can explain what his body is doing.

- Keep it simple. Healthy body awareness also helps keep toddlers safe later on.

- Say, "When you drink, the water goes through your body to make you strong, and then goes into a pocket called a bladder. When it is full, your brain will feel it and say it is time to empty."

Make sure you have potty tools: small toilets, insert seats, stools, wipes. These things help toddlers feel more relaxed when they are ready to sit. Be prepared for accidents. It can be months before this is perfected. Toddlers can wait too long or have trouble reading body cues. They are trying to integrate a lot of understanding and get it all into muscle memory. If you feel like you are going to yell or shame your child about an accident, try your best to stop. Not so easy to do, but it is easy to get into a negative cycle with toddlers where the worse they feel about an accident, the more they withhold; the more they withhold, the less they go and the more accidents they will have.

Forcing the issue usually does not work in the long run, no matter how angry we are with our toddler. Gently remind your toddler, even if it is through clenched teeth, that the next time he can try again to remember to use the toilet.

Be Cool

- When toddlers start to use the toilet intermittently, try not to ramp up your expectations. They are still practicing and integrating their emotional readiness with their body readiness. This takes time, sometimes months, to get in sync.

- Be matter-of-fact about what your toddler is doing. Let him know you noticed that he sat longer today, or tell him he can try tomorrow again.

The Lowdown on Pooping

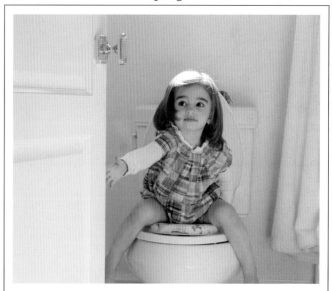

- Toddlers pee in the toilet before they move their bowels while sitting on the toilet. It takes most toddlers about 10 minutes to sit and relax enough to go when they are first starting.

- Try to have some good books in the bathroom, or let her pick a few she wants. If after 10 minutes she has not gone, try again later. Sometimes children who sit longer are disengaged from the process at hand.

ACTICE DOESN'T MAKE PERFECT

ut what it does do is give toddlers an opportunity to learn more about using the toilet

When we practice things, we begin to feel more matter-of-fact or comfortable with what is going to happen and what we need to do. Give your toddler some opportunities to do this. Speak your body awareness out loud sometimes. Say, "Oh, my body is telling me I have to pee now." Observation is often a underrated but powerful tool and can be very important.

Toddlers often like to come into the bathroom with you, so if you are comfortable, let them follow you in. Talk about what you are doing. Let them get some toilet paper. If they want to flush, let them try a few times. All of these things help a toddler imagine what it will be like for her to do them herself. If your toddler would like to practice pouring water from a

Using a Public Toilet

- Using a toilet in public feels and smells different, so try to bring a small insert when you are out.

- Do a practice flush before your toddler sits down to prepare him—public toilets are noisier.

- Try to be positive about using a public toilet, or at least pretend to be.

- Give some choices: Would you like to press the dryer button?

Can You Hold It?

- When you are traveling or running errands during toilet training, be prepared. Bring an extra diaper or two just in case. Bring wipes and hand sanitary solution.

- If your toddler gets upset about having an accident when she is out, tell her that it gets easier to plan ahead. Try not to say, "I told you to go before you left." Time does not work that way for toddlers.

cup into the toilet, encourage her to do so. Sometimes, if she wants to sit on the toilet, you can ask her if she wants to pour water in and let her pour it in between her legs.

Toddlers also get ready to use the toilet by reading stories that focus on the subject. Read these books together, and talk about poop and pee and how different children use the potty at different times. Making up stories about another toddler who just happens to be the same age or have the same name is a wonderful opportunity for toddlers to hear about themselves. Point out toilets at the park or store so your toddler can begin to understand that they are everywhere. Talk about hand washing. Let your toddler wash her hands with soap after you have visited the bathroom.

To Stand or Not to Stand

- Whether you are toilet training a boy or a girl, give them experience with your partner as well. It is important that toddlers know both of you can help when you are out.

- Little boys may be very interested in how to pee standing up. Let them choose, once they have mastered a little control over how to start and stop the flow.

Little Exercises Can Help

- When older toddlers or preschool children are practicing, they sometimes find it helpful to pour water from a cup between their legs. This simulation can help them feel more at ease.

- It is also helpful for children when they are using the big toilet to put a stool under their feet. It is important for them to feel stable while they are sitting.

TO REWARD OR NOT

Knowing your own toddler helps you determine whether she will benefit from rewards

Toddlers can feel overpressured to perform when they are rewarded for using the toilet, so it is important to decide if the short-term gain is going to come with challenges later on. Children, like all of us, like to hear praise. But when we are rewarded for doing something we are expected to do, it can be confusing. We are sending a mixed message to toddlers that they should be able to expect rewards for taking care of themselves.

Children and adults learn best when we want to accomplish something. And when we accomplish what we set out to do, it feels good. Praise can be different from rewarding but can also be a slippery slope for toddlers and parents because

Using Incentives

- Try to stick to small things—the road to bribery is a slippery slope.

- If your toddler likes stickers, use a fun setup. Draw a big green leaf, and when she pees in the toilet, let her add a bug sticker to the leaf. When that leaf is full, you can do another one and use the leaves to make a big tree.

- Give a cheer together—high five or fist pop.

- Time is important to toddlers and can be a powerful incentive. After they pee say, "Let's do something fun together. What would you like to play?"

Training with Stories

- Toileting books can be fun for toddlers. They like hearing about how everyone pees.

- Toddlers may also like to hear stories you make up while they sit. Make up a character, maybe an elephant that had a very big bathroom for her very special big bottom. Toddlers love this kind of thing and may be more willing to relax and sit for a while.

toddlers can expect it or begin to feel that everything they do is worthy of praise, which after a while does not feel comfortable. Try being descriptive when your toddler has done something positive so he can hear what he just did and feel the pride coming from within him. When you see your toddler smile after he has used the toilet, you can join him: Smile and say, "I am glad you are feeling happy. You took good care of yourself. I am happy too."

····· GREEN●LIGHT ·············

Say to your toddler, "Look at all the things you just did. You listened to your body. You stopped playing and went to the bathroom. You and I pulled down your pants and you peed in the toilet." Then watch the look on her face when she takes it all in.

Body Awareness

- When your toddler starts to use the toilet to move her bowels, more language will be needed. Say, "Muscles help you push. Your body will help you."

- Show toddlers how to wipe. They will still need your help to begin with, but when they are mostly clean, let them practice.

My Legs Won't Bend

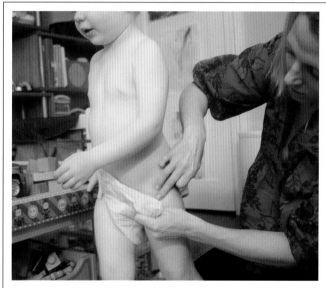

- Toddlers become very resistant to lying down for diaper changes once they start increasing body awareness. They resist relinquishing control over what happens, and this can make for a high-conflict time.

- Give your toddler a warning. When it is time for the change, let him hold the timer to see how fast the changing is.

- Try not to blame him for being slow in toilet training. He will get there.

EQUIPMENT FOR TOILET TRAINING

Items to have on hand when your toddler seems ready to use the toilet

Preparing for toilet training does not require a lot of equipment, but there are some items that can be helpful. Most importantly, if your child is going to do some sitting on the big toilet, she needs a stool under her feet. If she does not feel stable on the big seat, she will have a harder time relaxing to void.

You can purchase any number of freestanding potties to use next to the big toilet. This allows your toddler to sit while you are sitting or standing, even if it is with her clothes on. While she sits there, talk about what you are doing: wiping and flushing.

Having a toilet insert can be helpful for traveling or running

Potty Types

- The most important part of picking a potty seat is finding one your toddler feels comfortable with that works in your bathroom. Let him go with you to pick one out, and involve him in the process.

- Continue to be matter-of-fact about the purchase. You have a way to go, and this is just a marker, not the race.

Travel and Toilet Training

- There are many ways you can be prepared for toilet training when you travel. There are disposable paper covers for public toilets, potties that can be used in the car to avoid public toilets, and seats that insert.

- It can sometimes be helpful to have a few options, but try not to overdo it. Decide on the strategy that is best for your lifestyle and needs and then get the supplies you need that will support that.

errands once your toddler is actually doing some peeing on the toilet and you are trying to avoid some of the public seats. This will seem familiar and comfortable for her, and you will not have to worry about her touching the public seat.

It is also important to carry around moist wipes to help your toddler get clean. Your toddler will need help wiping for quite a while. This is a harder skill to manage than using the toilet itself. Some toddlers are more worried about getting their hands dirty, so they will be cautious.

Getting a Good Setup

- It is important to have a stool that is the right height for your toddler when she is learning to use the big toilet. If there is one that has adjustable heights, it will also work at the sink and then later on as she grows.

- Make sure you use a bleach-water solution to spray off all equipment from time to time. Germs spread easily, and keeping everything sanitized can help reduce traveling bugs.

Green Products

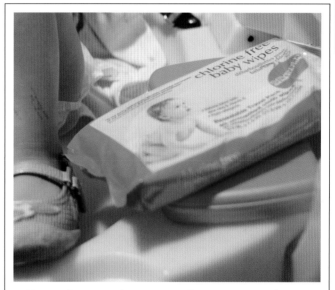

- More and more products are being created that are green. This is a good opportunity to support environmental issues and teach your toddler about them as well.

- Costs are coming down on green products, so shop around. Sometimes buying in bulk directly from the manufacturer helps. Put up a flyer at your school or day care to see if there are others who may want to go in on cost.

SAYING GOOD-BYE TO DIAPERS

The final step in potty training is your toddler's decision to start using underwear

Diapers provide toddlers with security and comfort. When they are learning to use the toilet, it may take months before they are ready to switch to underwear. Before you introduce your toddler to underwear, give him some time before and after his bath to go without anything. This gives him time to get more comfortable with not wearing a diaper.

Point out the differences between underpants and diapers. Remember that language for the process is important. Let your toddler know that when he is ready to use the toilet all the time, he will have underpants. Purchase a package or two of underpants and let him wear them around the house. Give him a choice. If he wants to switch over to a diaper after

Pediatricians Need to Know

Health Concerns to Share with Your Doctor:

- Big increase or decrease in urine flow or bowel movements

- Bowel movements that are too hard to pass

- Your toddler is in pain

Transitioning to Underwear

- The transition to underwear is a big step for many toddlers. When you have had multiple days of dryness, start seeing if your toddler would like to try underpants for a short period of time.

- Since she is used to the bulk of a diaper or pull-up, she may be surprised at how she feels when her pee is coming because she may be more aware of a little leakage. Try to find underwear that is easy to pull up for toddler hands.

a minute or two, let him have the choice. Some toddlers will even want to wear their underwear over their diaper. Try to be flexible.

It is also important, once you switch to underwear, to make sure the rest of your toddler's clothing is easy to pull down. She needs to be able to get both her underwear and pants down far enough that she does not wet them when using the toilet.

If your toddler is dry during the day, the last frontier is the night. You can remind her to use the toilet before bed. If her diaper continues to be dry in the morning, you can begin to use pull-ups or training pants at night. If these stay dry, your toddler can usually manage to stay dry all night. Health problems can change things, even for a toddler who has been dry for months. Keep a few extra diapers around just in case.

School Rules

- If your school has a policy about toilet training, you may have to consider other options. The more pressure children feel, the more you risk toileting problems.

- Children train differently. As parents, we need to find the balance between pressure and encouragement. Talk to your doctor or other professional if you think your child is holding and becoming constipated.

Effects of Illness

- When toddlers are ill, their systems will be off. This may be a time of more accidents. Sometimes children, once they are trained, get more upset than parents do when they soil themselves.

- Help your toddler understand what is going on in his body. Explain that sometimes his poop is softer or smells differently, and that it will change when he feels better.

AGE-APPROPRIATE GUIDELINES

Toddlers crave limits, and it is important to set age-appropriate guidelines for them

Toddlers between 12 and 36 months have different social, emotional, and cognitive understandings of the world. At up to 12 months, or at least until your toddler is moving on her own two feet, we are pretty happy with what our babies are doing. We are mostly in control of their world, so if we want to keep them in the living room, it usually happens. Once toddlers begin to move, they want to go everywhere, and the number of things that can be dangerous or inappropriate for them to play with increases.

Toddlers have to get used to limit-setting. It is not an easy task for any of us, and the groundwork gets set during the toddler years. We are not born with a switch to shut off

Guidelines for Limit-Setting

- Teach your toddler what he can and cannot do.

- Help your toddler soothe himself.

- Label your feelings and his.

- Help your toddler solve the problem.

Modeling Is Still Important

- Toddlers in 12- to 18-month range are aware that what they want may not be possible. Redirection is still a good tool, but now you also begin to name your toddler's feelings and empathize with her frustration.

- Modeling in every phase of development is still one of the most important leaning mechanisms for young children. If you are learning these tools at the same time as your toddler, go slow. You can do this differently from the way you were raised.

our impulsive behavior, but we are born with the ability to learn over time how to slow our impulses and adapt our behaviors.

Toddlers are learning about self-control, the experience of having a strong feeling or desire, and the ability to manage themselves when they do not get what they want. Like almost everything your toddler learns, this happens in small ways. This is a good time to talk with your partner about what each of you thinks is appropriate guidance.

Reading Your Toddler

- Toddlers become increasingly expressive as they get older. Redirecting may become less successful. Paying attention to your toddler's state of mind, temperament, persistence, and flexibility will help guide you when you are working through difficult times.

- When you say no to your toddler, use an "I" message. Say, "I do not want you to touch that. I will say no again. I do not want you to touch that." For some toddlers, this is an easier way to hear the limit.

Triggers

- Language, both how toddlers understand things and how they express themselves, is more relevant now. Thinking ahead about what triggers your toddler will help you avoid difficult situations for her.

- You cannot avoid everything, but you can reduce the number of times you feel things are heating up.

UNDERSTANDING TODDLER EMOTIONS

When toddlers have to deal with limit-setting, their emotions can go to a whole new place

Toddlers start saying "no" as a way to let you know that they are beginning to understand their world and want some say in things: I can have this. I do not want that. The world is no longer black-and-white, and they are experimenting with new and very complicated concepts. Toddlers cannot reason yet, so they use "no" to declare independence, desire,

and some healthy aggression. When your toddler is upset he cannot have the remote, we can be tempted to grab it away. But what we are saying when we do is, "It's mine. I am bigger." This cuts to the chase sometimes but leaves a toddler seeing that the way not to feel bad anymore is to grab what you want. When he takes that behavior out into the real world, it

Intensifying Emotions

- Toddler emotions can get bigger and more intense over time.

- They cannot feel gratified every time we interact with them. They feel internally disorganized, and this can be reflected through anger or sadness.

- Toddlers cannot easily reset themselves when they are in the middle of these feelings. They do not yet have the developmental skills to just stop.

Toddlers Still Need Comfort

- When toddlers are crying, they need comfort, but that does not mean they can have everything they want.

- Let your toddler know you see she is sad. Tell her you can help her. This may mean just sitting with her on your lap.

- We cannot solve every problem for them as much as we wish we could, so sometimes helping them is just being there.

does not work well.

What we can start to do is identify our toddler's emotions. Say, "You are mad that you cannot have that. I know you love that remote. How can I help you feel better? Can I hold you? Can we find something else to hold?" A toddler response to this might be, "You are right. I am mad, and thank-you for helping me," although it is more likely to be screaming and crying. Our job is then to stand by and offer to help again by comforting or finding something else the two of you can do together. The challenge of all this is that we have to feel okay about letting our toddlers be sad or upset without being indifferent to them. Our job as parents is to help our children know that part of loving them is teaching them to cope with limits.

What Happened?

- As toddlers become more aware of language, you can use more information. You can talk more about what happened and why they felt sad.

- Toddlers cannot often really explain what led up to this feeling. You can help connect the dots. Say, "You felt sad when I asked you to put your blanket in the crib. You love your blanket. We can get it at nap time."

Empathy Goes a Long Way

- Acknowledging toddlers' feelings is how they learn to control their experiences with disappointment or limit-setting.

- When we want children to learn how to read, we sing the alphabet and read stories to them. Teaching children how to have inner discipline or the ability to make healthy choices requires time and tools.

- Wanting our children to behave is what most parents hope for. How you get there takes as much work from you as your toddler.

TALKING TO YOUR TODDLER

Talking to a toddler about her feelings can take time and lots and lots of repetition

When our toddlers begin to use language, they will express themselves in many ways. You begin to see how they think about the world, and it is mostly magical. When we help toddlers with their emotions, we are trying to help them cope with the ups and downs of their feelings. When they were babies, our job was to soothe and comfort them so they would feel safe, and now we are saying, "I cannot always make that happen for you."

When you are talking to your toddler, try to keep it simple. Keep naming the feeling you think they are having just the way you name the trucks and cars that go by. Be as matter-of-fact as possible—sometimes this works better than at

Regulating Mood

- Some toddlers need help to develop more assertive language, and some toddlers need help slowing it down.

- Stay near when your toddler cannot be consoled—he needs to feel you close.

- Use the way you understand your toddler to provide helpful tools to manage feelings.

- Temperament and environment play a role; reflect on what is happening with your toddler.

Stay Connected

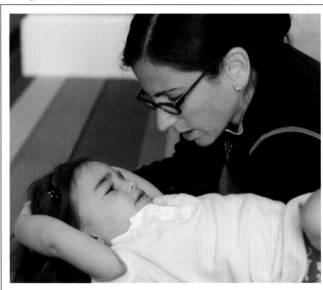

- When you are talking to your toddler, it is important to connect with her first. Say, "I know you are angry about what happened, and I am here to help you."

- If you yell from another room, she is less likely to respond to what you are saying. Let her know that you understand that she got mad because her brother took the shovel but that she still cannot hit. Help her find words to talk to her brother. Stay close.

other times. Keep your expectations at the age and stage of your toddler. Toddlers don't know that hitting hurts when they are 18 months old, so you need to explain why their friend is crying.

Help explain consequences. Say, "When your friend grabbed the toy, you got sad." Give your toddler words to help: "Would you like this shovel instead, or should we go ask your friend to trade?" Be clear. Toddlers get more confused when you vacillate. If you are not sure if your decision is right, you can correct it later on.

Toddlers need to hear this kind of language a lot. They need time to understand that words can be helpful. They also need to see that you will help them with their feelings the way you help them stay physically safe. When our children are learning how to walk, we focus on helping them feel strong. Each fall is greeted with, "You can do this—try again." Emotional coaching is no different.

Public Parenting

- Toddlers of all ages can show distress and anger in many ways. When they are out in public, it can be harder to be as consistent.

- Keep it simple when you are out. Sometimes we say more than we need to because we are worried about what others might think. The most you may be able to do is identify what your toddler is feeling and contain your own feelings as best you can.

Normal Aggression

- As they get older, toddlers may begin to use more aggressive behaviors. Some of these behaviors are normal but unacceptable. Try to help your toddler know the difference.

- Say, "I know you threw the toy because you were mad. When you throw toys they can hurt someone. If you get that mad again, you can hit the pillow or tell your friend to stop. I will help you find a different way to show your angry feeling."

TEMPER TANTRUMS

Helping your toddler calm himself down and staying steady

When your toddler is lying on the sidewalk, screaming and throwing himself around, you might think, "How in the world can I get this child up and out of here without making more of a scene?" The mixture of helplessness and hopelessness that you feel is, in fact, what a toddler having a tantrum is feeling.

What started out as anger, sadness, disappointment, or frustration for your toddler has escalated into a feeling of powerlessness. Toddlers need our help more than ever to pull themselves together, which will look different every time. Sometimes we are not in a good place to help our toddlers, and sometimes our toddlers are overtired and less equipped to cope with the process.

Make sure you stay near when your toddler is losing it. Even if you are embarrassed, stay steady. Wait quietly for a few

Coping with Temper Tantrums

- When meltdowns happen, your toddler is already past the point of being able to pull it back together again.

- Don't discipline your toddler for the tantrum. She cannot control herself.

- Help your toddler get to a safe space so she does not hurt herself.

- You won't be able to reason with your toddler in this emotional whirlwind. Wait it out and then begin to problem-solve.

- Toddlers can be scared of the intensity of their own feelings when they are in the throes of a temper tantrum.

Identify Stressors

- If your toddler is having more and more temper tantrums, try to think about what may be going on in his life. Some toddlers, as they drop their nap, have a hard time pacing themselves throughout the day. This can result in increased frustration.

- If a parent has been traveling a lot or is busier than usual, this can be a contributing factor. Sometimes when we identify the real triggers, things can go more smoothly because we can correct something.

minutes, then ask your toddler calmly if you can hold him to help him feel better. If he starts screaming, tell him you will be here waiting to help when he is ready. When he is able to accept your help or begins to self-soothe, try to let him relax. At home, talk about what happened. Toddlers will have meltdowns, but you can minimize them when you can model coping skills.

Read Books about Feelings

- Read books to your toddler about angry feelings. Talk together about what he has experienced. Discuss what the character in the book does when he is angry.

- When your toddler handles something well, such as not hitting his little sister, point it out. Say, "I saw you stop your hand before you hit your sister."

I Feel Like a Volcano

- This can be a good time to use visuals. Talk about how anger can make us feel so hot that we need to cool down.

- Ask your toddler what else gets hot. Ask him what he does when he is hot—such as blow on his soup or get out of the sun.

- Toddlers are still concrete in their thinking and can use pictures to help with imagining how to go about an emotional task.

WHICH BATTLES TO TACKLE?

When dealing with toddlers who are developing emotional and social skills, focus on what you can manage

Toddlers are so busy that if you try to focus on all of their challenging behaviors, you will be more exhausted than you probably already are—and that is pretty tired. It is important that you pick one or two behaviors at a time that you want to work on. List all the ones that seem to either bother you the most or create the most difficulty for your toddler. Once

you have that list, prioritize the things you want to start with. For some parents it is throwing food, for others hitting, and for others it is whining. The list is endless. Continue to think about what is developmentally appropriate to expect from your toddler so you do not set him or yourself up for more frustration.

Ways to Help Toddlers

- Make your environment toddler friendly—try to remove temptations.

- Keep your errands down to one a day.

- Try to have 20 minutes a day when he is the leader—this helps him be a better follower when you need him to be.

- Toddler temperament is different—pace your day around your toddler's ability to manage transitions.

- Act out some of your toddler's challenges in play. Say, "My fire truck does not want to go into the firehouse."

Pick Your Battles

- When we sit down ahead of time with our partners, we can determine what we want to focus on at any given time. We all have limited time and resources and energy, so work with what you think your toddler needs the most help with.

- You can get to the other issues in time. Sometimes, as toddlers mature chronologically, behaviors that are of concern to us just drop away.

Once you have figured out where you want to start, take a few days to think about all the situations that seem to make this behavior come out. Are there times of day or situations that seem to increase these behaviors? Once you have identified the situations, you are more likely to anticipate the behavior and deal with it effectively. Try to separate what you have control over and what your toddler will have control over. If going on errands never ends well, there is not much a toddler can do to change the trigger, so think of ways you might want to do things differently. Once you have changed as much as you can, you can begin to help your toddler with his part.

Toddler frustrations and temper tantrums cannot be totally avoided no matter what we do. They are a part of typical development. The goal is to provide coping skills for when these situations arise.

Be Consistent

- Every family decides what is important to them. Make sure that you are consistent.

- Keep the same expectations and same consequences when you are tackling a behavioral concern. Before you tackle it, think about your toddler's temperament so you can predict places where you might run into difficulties.

- Use play and story times to talk about behaviors and feelings. This can help set the stage.

Emotional Safety

- Having safe environments emotionally and physically can actually reduce some of the meltdowns that your toddler may experience. When toddlers know that it is safe to express their feelings, they learn to release tension or stress as they go along.

- If toddlers learn to suppress their feelings, they will erupt—it is the law of nature.

213

KEEPING YOUR FEELINGS IN CHECK
Learning how to identify your own anger triggers will help your toddler

Before we have children, it is hard to imagine how tired or frustrated we are going to feel. We think we will do it differently and better than everyone else. The hard truth is that until we have children, it is impossible to know what will trigger our emotions in ways that can be hurtful to our children.

As parents now, we are either modeling the way we were parented or avoiding the way we were parented. What this means in practical terms is that we are trying to re-parent ourselves and parent our toddlers at the same time. It is this combination of emotions that can lead us to say and do things to our children that are physically or emotionally hurtful. We are all capable of doing this regardless of background.

Examining Our Own Childhoods

- Sometimes our other life experiences impact the way we react to feeling angry with our children. If you know this is true for you or are worried about a reaction you had to your child, it may take some courage to begin to figure out what is going on.

- Try doing some journaling. Writing down what you are feeling helps. You may be surprised at the intensity of your feelings, but feelings are just that: feelings. You can learn how to choose the actions you take.

Learning Together

- The more you help your toddler learn emotional expressiveness, the more you will learn, too. Be open to being a student at the same time you are a teacher.

- If you think you are getting too close to physically hurting your toddler, have a plan. It is wise to have a friend who can talk you down, and to put space between you and your toddler: a thought, a door, or an image—whatever works for you.

Learn your triggers and avoid them whenever possible. Try to remember that your reaction in the moment is a mix of old feelings within you and new feelings about your child's behavior. Try to react to the here and now. See if you can reduce an overreaction by 10 percent at first, and keep increasing the amount over time. Try to build in rest time for yourself once a week.

Squeezing in breaks can mean using your lunch hour to take a nap or read a book. A few nights a month, go to bed when your toddler does and wake up an hour earlier to have tea and look out the window. Last but not least, be gentle to yourself. Forgive yourself when you don't do things the wished for way. Try again tomorrow.

We All Have Strengths

- It is important to remind yourself that when your toddler is having a hard time, it is only one part of him you are both struggling with.

- Make a list of the other things you love or like about your child, and focus on these things. Build on your toddler's strengths. Reach out. Sometimes friends are not the best support in this situation, so find someone who can really help you puzzle this out.

Make Time for Emotion Coaching

- Know your parenting style and try to add coaching techniques.

- Separate your agenda from what is an appropriate agenda for your toddler's developmental stage.

- Have a mental understanding of your toddler's day-to-day life so you can plan accordingly.

- Think about things from your child's perspective, not just your own.

- Sometimes we are too busy to do emotion coaching, but do the best you can. Some of the time is better than none of the time.

TIME TO YOURSELF

Making time for yourself is hard to do, but the payoff for you and your toddler is significant

When we have children, it becomes very difficult to make time to take care of ourselves. We are busy with child care, which is nonstop, our responsibilities at home, work outside the home, and maintaining ties with friends and family. Parents often say it is just not possible to find time for themselves because when their toddler goes to sleep, they have to get ready for the next day. That is true, but the most important part of readiness is self-care. It allows you to feel more rested, which means you will have better and more effective coping skills.

Much of the hard stuff of parenting is dealing with the emotional ups and downs your children are experiencing.

Ideas for Taking Time

• Wake up a few minutes earlier in the morning to drink your coffee.

• Bring your toddler's high chair outside at lunch so you can sit outside together and breathe the air.

• Lay down on the floor when your toddler is playing and take a few good stretches and breathe.

• Have afternoon tea.

• Buy yourself some flowers each week and keep them somewhere you can look at them, pause and remind yourself that it does not just get harder, it gets easier, too. Life ebbs and flows.

What Do You Need?

• Relaxing means different things to different parents. For some it is listening to music, and for others it is a night out with friends.

• Take some time to list the things that help you relax. We all know how to come up with the obstacles to getting to those places, so try finding solutions.

When you are overwhelmed, it is much more difficult to do. We encourage toddlers to learn how to take good care of themselves, and we need to model the same behavior.

Finding time for yourself daily is not always possible, but finding time once a week is. The first step is not just hoping you will find time for yourself, but making it a priority and following through on your intention. When we intend to do something, we take more accountability for making it happen. Make a list of things you feel you have to do before you take time for yourself, and prioritize your list. Then imagine you have only a few hours left in your life and must choose only one thing to accomplish. Decide what matters most.

Making time for yourself may mean letting go of something else. Leaving your toddler's clean clothes in the laundry basket means time not spent folding and putting them away so you can use that time to read.

A Mini Getaway

- If a getaway weekend is on your list but is not going to happen any time soon, get a sitter for two hours, drive to a park, and bring tea, music, books, or anything else you want.

- Climb in your backseat if you want extreme privacy and say: This is practice for the real deal and allows us to feel that we, even in limited ways, recognize the value of self.

Importance of Self-Care

- Your physical health depends on it.
- Your emotional health depends on it.
- Your partner relationship depends on it.
- Your parent-child relationship depends on it.

TIME FOR PARTNERS

Our relationships with our partners need time and attention as much as those with our children do

Transitioning to parenthood takes time and energy. We can prepare for the physical environment and imagine what some of the changes will be like for us emotionally, but we cannot foresee all the ways it will impact us as a couple. We often are so focused on keeping our heads above water that we are exhausted and unable to find time for our relationships

with each other. When you make this a shared priority, you will have taken a first step in some of the most important parenting you will do.

Time together is important for many reasons. When you spend time together you can stay emotionally connected. You can share stories about your children, talk about ways to

Importance of Time Together

- More time for problem-solving, which may mean less conflict.

- More empathy for the other.

- More sharing of responsibilities.

- More intimacy.

- More opportunities to laugh together in the face of the hard work of parenting.

Finding Meaningful Time

- Time together means different things to each partner. Try to build in one night or day a month that gives both of you some of what you want.

- Partner time may be better on a weekend morning,

when you are a little more rested. Sometimes early morning sitters are more available. Go to breakfast together and ask your sitter to take your toddler out to the park. Then go home and climb back into bed together.

change things in the household, follow up with each other, resolve disagreements, and have physical intimacy. If this is not a part of your everyday routine from the beginning, it becomes increasingly difficult to find time when you really need it, which is often when we are at our breaking points.

Partner relationships take work and time. When you maintain a strong connection to each other, you model intimacy, problem-solving, communication, and more to your toddlers. Physical intimacy can decrease significantly during the early years of parenting. A woman's sexual drive is impacted by fatigue. By not building in dependable time together, we sometimes choose to be task oriented rather than relaxing together. You may not have much time for physical intimacy, but make sure you have some. Talk about it, be silly about it, flirt. If you plan on one night a week to be together sexually, you will actually see it less as an obligation and more as something to look forward to. Let your partner know that the best foreplay might be help cleaning up the kitchen that night.

Added Stressors

- If there is additional stress beyond children and work, finding time is more challenging.

- This may be a time when exchanging e-mails more regularly and talking about feelings, worries, and hopes may be all you can do. When we are letting each other know how important we are to each other, it gives us the reserve to keep going.

Keeping the Connection

- Create some time-management connections with each other. Purchase a white plastic tablecloth and permanent marker to keep nearby, and write notes to each other regularly.

- You will be surprised how each of you will become curious about how the other is reacting to what is written. Work through a conflict—writing can slow down our rage. Flirt; be funny.

MEDIA EXPOSURE

Fast-paced technology can have both a positive and negative impact on your toddler

How much television our toddlers should watch, and how much computer time they should have, are questions parents are faced with more and more as our children are exposed to so many kinds of media. Sometimes we use the media to buy us time. A little television viewing can give you time for a quick bathroom trip, or a chance to put on your clothes or make dinner. But how do we figure out how much or what our children should watch?

It is estimated that children between two and five years of age spend approximately 25 hours a week in front of a movie or program on television. At this rate, by 18 years of age a child will have spent more time in front of the TV than

Technology Advances

- Our children will always be ahead of us in technology because it changes constantly.

- If you use the computer as part of your day-to-day life at home, your toddler will be curious. If you decide to let her sit with you, look for interactive sites that you can do together.

- Although your toddler is not going to surf the Web yet, start early learning how to safeguard her. Predators are thorough; be equally if not more thorough.

But I Love That Show!

- Television can be the best and the worst. It can help us out in times of need by buying us a few minutes, but it can also become a way to model avoidance.

- If you find yourself using television more, spend a minute to try to understand why.

- Children of all ages have difficulty at times turning off the set, so be ready to do some engaged playtime to help transition them.

in school. In addition, by four years of age the increase in violence in programming goes up by almost a third.

One of the best ways to judge how much time to let your toddler watch television is to determine the current ratio of TV watching to reading and indoor and outdoor playtime. If you don't like the results, you can begin to increase each of the latter activities with your toddler by 20 percent, which will automatically decrease the use of media. This will make the transition a lot easier. Also, make sure you have watched what your toddler is seeing so you can talk about it or eliminate it.

Choosing DVDs

- DVDs can be another way to get some time as a parent, but it is important to be aware of what your toddler is seeing.

- Toddlers cannot separate fantasy from reality, so scenes that show death or fear can be confusing.

- Watch to see if a scene is mentally invading their play as they express worry or concern.

- Look for DVDs of your toddler's favorite storybooks. These are easy to monitor because you already know the content.

GREEN ● LIGHT

When you need time to do something, try using a story tape to keep your toddler occupied. Libraries are great sources for these.

Media and Children

- Evaluate regularly how much or why you are using media. Sometimes it is just habit.

- As they get older, children need more help transitioning from technology. Give them a transition plan.

- Pay close attention to what your children are interested in. If they love bugs, use the technology to support their interests, not the other way around.

- Try to avoid eating in front of the television. It can be a contributing factor to obesity later on in life.

EVERYDAY FAMILY LIFE

221

CLEANUP TIMES

Helping toddlers learn to clean up is about modeling and organizing things simply

Once you have children, the amount of stuff you collect is unbelievable. Trying to keep it organized is almost impossible, but helping toddlers learn to clean up after themselves models social responsibility, which leads to healthier self-esteem for them.

One of the best ways to do this is through modeling teamwork. Cleanup for most people is more fun when we are working together, so see if you can build group cleanup time into your family routines. For very young toddlers who are not pulling things out on their own yet, make cleanup a part of your play routine. Talk about what you are doing—sing a cleanup song. When you are done, stand back, high

Organizing Storage

- Try having lots of bins with simple titles and matching pictures. While it is nice sometimes to get all the pieces back in a set, part of what toddlers love is mix and match.

- Rotate toys so not everything is down at once. Change playthings seasonally the way you would your clothes.

- Keep things reachable for toddlers with low shelves and baskets.

- If multiple pieces make you crazy, try using them on a mat. Then you can just roll it up and dump for easy cleanup.

It's Cleanup Time!

- Come up with a good cleanup song. Toddlers like rituals, so make this a part of the activity. Talk about what you are going to do after cleanup is done.

- If you are cleaning up because it is bedtime, focus on your special under-the-star time together. This gives you some shared purpose.

five, and talk about how nice it feels to have everything clean.

Once your toddler gets older, help him put things away a few times a day. Talk about how nice it was to play with the blocks, and explain they will be ready for him later on. Try doing some toy washing on a weekend once a month or so. Give toddlers a squirt bottle, and let them wipe and spray away. Remind them afterward that it was fun doing the job together.

Getting Cleanup Started

- Toddlers have a limited ability to focus, so if there are pieces scattered everywhere, they will become distracted.

- Do a little cleanup prep— put most of the blocks away and then start to clean up and have them help. As they get older, reduce the amount of prep you do but still make the work age-appropriate.

- The long-term goal is to make this a part of their lives, not to grade how much they did on any given night.

Toddlers Still Love Cleaning

- Have toddlers participate in different types of cleanup tasks. They like to help with dishes, put away clothes, shake out the dustpan, and water plants.

- Use language. Say, "This is so much easier when we do this together. I am glad we are on the same team."

MANAGING YOUR TIME
Managing time seems like an oxymoron once you have children, but it can be done

Managing time becomes much easier when you take the time to see what it is that you really need to do. When we do not break down our work into priorities, we are quickly overwhelmed. Start by listing everything you need to do at home, at work, and for parenting. On each list make three columns: have to get it done or die, need to get it done or

be frustrated, nice to get it done but no real consequences if it isn't. Now go back and circle the musts. If your partner is willing to do this with you, see if your lists are comparable. Sometimes we are doing things we think our partners expect us to do, but in fact they don't.

See which of these tasks your toddler can help you with. Do

Time-Management Tips

• If you work, use lunch hours to accomplish some of your tasks.

• If you shop during the day, leave a cooler with ice in your car so you can store perishables.

• Eliminate clothes or linens that need to be ironed. Use a clothing steamer or a spray bottle to remove wrinkles.

• Store your breakable treasures for a while until your toddler is past the age of taking everything apart.

Be Imaginative

• Doing laundry can also be a playtime with your toddler. Go on a bear hunt looking for dirty clothes, and hide them together in the washer.

• Doing some tasks with your child helps the day go more smoothly, but not all tasks are possible with toddlers.

• Sometimes doing the grocery shopping by yourself is more efficient and provides both alone time for a parent or some distance from parenting worries.

toy cleanup together. Simplify meal plans—toddlers like simple. Go grocery shopping early with a travel mug of coffee when stores are empty and you are not yet exhausted and can think. If you need to take your toddler with you, bring her in her pajamas. Do a menu plan ahead of time so you are not taking time to figure out what to have for dinner each day.

Do You Really Have To?

- Try to limit your must-do list to two things a day. When our lists get longer, we end up feeling that we really did not get much accomplished, which leaves us feeling more exhausted and overwhelmed.

- Reframing can be a great help when we have young children. It is much easier to change a frame than change an entire day or week.

Prioritizing Helps Manage Time

- You cannot manage your time until you figure out for yourself what that means.

- There are very few things in life that have to be done immediately. Sometimes just seeing why you are feeling so driven will result in ultimately helping you reduce the pressure, which gives you more time.

- Worrying and avoiding are big time-grabbers.

CREATING FAMILY RITUALS
Meaningful family times have long-lasting positive effects on children

It is helpful to start some family rituals early on. Like everything else with parenting, keep it simple. Maybe you will decide to do an early Saturday morning walk or a dance party every Sunday afternoon with graham crackers and juice. The most important thing is not what you do, but the fact that you prioritize the time on your calendar to do something as a family. These times should be free of television and phones. They should be set in stone so that barring emergencies, everyone remembers not to double book. These times can be short—30 minutes at first is good. Make work or stressful situations off-limit topics for these special times.

Take turns planning family times. If it is winter and conditions

Family Time Ideas

- Pancake walk—make some pancakes and bring them along on a walk.

- Fill a place in your yard with water puddles and go out with boots and splash away together. New walkers love this.

- Put down a bunch of long and winding masking tape roads on your living room floor together, and get out all your toddler's trucks and cars. Eat a snack off the back of a big dump truck together.

- Build a fort under your dining table; have flashlights and sing some songs together.

Less Can Be More

- Complicated family times are more apt to fall apart. Keep it simple. Once your toddler is school age, you may have to be more creative as their activities build up.

- A 30-minute picnic in your car may be as good as it gets at times, but if you have started rituals early with your toddler, she will continue to value and look forward to these times.

are bad and you cannot do what you had hoped, build an indoor sledding slope with cushions and sit on paper plates to slide down. Try taking pictures of these times so you can hang them up and talk about how much fun you have every Saturday. Toddlers will look forward to this time and be excited about the opportunity to have uninterrupted fun with everyone. Talk about this time as your "family time," so it is marked differently verbally for your toddler.

As your toddlers get older, these times will create memories of family. Day-to-day life is hard, so having time when there is no competing for attention teaches children the importance of time together. Have fun; be silly. When you end family time, help your toddler with the transition. As your toddler gets older, you can also use these times to talk about more serious issues such as different feelings they may be having.

Family Time Can Be Anything

- When you have more than one child, especially a baby and a toddler, family time can have different challenges.

- These times may end up being shorter. Still call it family time, and put it on the schedule.

- Announce it. Say, "I am so glad it is Sunday because after we get dressed it is family time." Let your toddler know the plan. Ask her what she thinks the baby can do to be part of family time.

Time Alone

- In addition to family time, it is also important for you to have time with each of your children alone.

- Often we divide and conquer—one parent and one child—but try to plan once a month when you have time together with each of your children. This helps you get to know them better and provides opportunities where they do not have to compete with each other.

227

RESOURCES

Chapter 1

There has been a great deal of important research on the brain and how toddlers feel, learn, and think. Stanley Greenspan's work on developing floor time for parents and educators is a philosophy and a technique that has guided and informed much of my work with young children. His books, DVDs, and articles will provide you with helpful ideas and information about floor time. **www.stanley greenspan.com.**

John Gottman's work as a researcher and family therapist has provided great insight into my emotional work with children. Both as a couple's therapist and for parenting support, he has guided families to a greater understanding of emotional behaviors with our children. **www.gottman.com.**

Doug Davies works as an educator, clinician, and researcher and has great insights into development for practitioners. *Child Development A Practitioner's Guide* is an invaluable book for anyone who works with children.

If you are interested in understanding more about "goodness of fit," read *Temperament and Development* by Alexander Thomas and Stella Chess.

There are many wonderful books on all aspects of parenting. I have listed ones that I like, but the key is finding ones you like and using as much of the guidance as you need or want.

Chapter 2

Good resources for developmental information include:

The American Academy of Pediatrics, **www.aap.org.**

Zero to Three, **www.zerotothree.org.**

For more information on emotion coaching, try these resources:

Raising an Emotionally Intelligent Child: The Heart of Parenting by John Gottman with Joan Declaire. Also available on DVD.

Your Child from One to Two and Two to Three by Louise Bates Ames. An easy, wonderful read.

Chapter 3

If you are looking for good information on sleep, feeding toddlers, and routines that work, go to **www.swellbeing.org.** They provide low-cost and informative online Web seminars in the evening.

Another great resource for inexpensive and good books is Scholastic Books, **www.scholastic.com.**

The Best Behavior series by Free Spirit Publishing consists of books on many toddler behaviors—great colors, easy language.

Chapter 6

The National Association for the Education of Young Children has a great Web site for learning more about child care, including locating accredited centers. **www.NAEYC.org.**

A good read based on longitudinal research on what children think of working mothers is *Ask the Children: What America's Children Really Think About Working Parents* by Ellen Galinsky. This will ease the guilt.

Chapter 4

Ellyn Satter's book on nutrition, *Child of Mine: Feeding with Love and Sense*, is a helpful way to avoid power struggles.

It is important to know how to use an EpiPen if your toddler has allergies; see **www.epipen.com.**

Allergy information and recipes can be found at **www.kidswith foodallergies.org.**

Chapter 5

Check out your local library for information on toddler reading groups. Libraries also often have lists of the best board books for toddlers and preschoolers.

www.Amazon.com is a good source for used books, especially favorites that are out of print.

Chapter 7

If you are concerned about developmental delays, talk to your pediatrician and check out the early-intervention programs in your area. If your toddler needs services, they are provided by the state at no cost.

Chapter 8

Some of the best information on car seat safety can be found on the American Academy of Pediatrics Web site, **www.aap.org.** Also check out **www.carsafety.org.**

Chapter 9

For the best allergy Web sites, go to **www.bestallergysites.com.**

For green products for packing lunches, check out **http://store .kidsserve.com.**

Chapter 10

Read *Caring Spaces, Learning Places* by Jim Greenman. This is a wonderful book that will trigger your imagination about creating spaces in your home no matter what the size.

Chapter 11

Here are some very good books, even if you only read a chapter a month:

If you are concerned about how much you seem to be pushing your child into activities, read David Elkind's book, *The Hurried Child.* It helps parents understand the need to help children feel less overstimulated.

Siblings Without Rivalry: How to Help Your Children Live Together So You Can Live Too by Adele Faber and Elaine Mazlish.

The Emotional Life of the Toddler by Alicia Lieberman.

Chapter 12

A very good Web site for understanding how children read is **www .readingrockets.org.** It provides developmental guidelines and lists of great books for children.

Chapter 13

www.nycmusichouse.com is an interesting and helpful Web site to learn about how to help your child become more musical.

When your toddler is ready for his first bike, check out **www.ibike .org** for good safety information.

www.babyswimming.com is a good information source for toddlers and water safety.

Chapter 14

For some fun cooking activities for toddlers, check out **www.familyplayandlearn.com/toddlercooking**.

If you are not sure about nutrition and want to learn more, go to **www.sparkpeople.com**. This is a great site to understand how to balance meals for yourself and your family.

Obesity is important to understand. Go to **www.kidshealth.org/parent/general/body** for information.

Chapter 15

Check out Bev Bos's books on art, music, finger play, and more. Her ideas are fun and easy. She uses everyday objects such as toilet plungers to paint with, and offers great ideas for the outdoors.

To make play dough: Mix 1 cup flour, $1/4$ cup salt, and 2 tablespoons cream of tarter in a pot. Stir in $1/2$ teaspoon oil, 1 cup cold water, and food coloring (natural or otherwise). Turn on heat and stir constantly until it thickens. This will take about 10 minutes. It will be sticky at first, but it will firm up. After it is a little cooler, knead and store or play! This is a small batch, so double if you want more.

Chapter 16

Learning the differences between boys and girls is important. Watch the video *Raising Cain: Boys in Focus,* which can be ordered from PBS. **www.pbs.org/opb/raisingcain/.** It is great for setting up parent discussions.

Chapter 17

www.pottytrainingstuff.com is a comprehensive site on supplies, including a good selection of potty books.

Inside Your Body is a good book to help older toddlers take a peek inside. You can even see the poop.

Chapter 18

There are lot of good books about feelings available. Here are a few:

I Can Share, No Biting!, and *No Hitting!* all by Karen Katz.

When Sophie Gets Angry—Really Really Angry… by Molly Bang.

Mommy, I Want to Sleep in Your Bed! by Harriet Ziefert.

Chapter 19

These books may be helpful resources:

The Seven Principles for Making Marriage Work by John Gottman and Nan Silver.

Sex Matters for Women: A Complete Guide to Taking Care of Your Sexual Self by Sallie Foley, Sally A. Kope, and Dennis P. Sugrue.

The Dance of Anger and *The Dance of Intimacy* by Harriet Lerner.

If you need to understand more about anger and its impact on relationships, go to **www.helpguide.org/mental/domestic-violence-abuse-help.**

PAINT & PLAYDOUGH RECIPES

These are not meant to be eaten by todders but will not hurt them so painting becomes more fun for both of you. You can substitue natural food dyes if you prefer.

Jello Finger Paint

1 cup cornstarch
¾ cup cold water and ¼ cup cold water
2 cups hot water
1 envelope of gelatin
½ cup clear dishwashing soap
2 cups of unsweetened kool aid

In a saucepan, blend ¾ cup cold water and cornstarch. Add 2 cups hot water. Heat until boiling stirring constantly. Remove from heat. Mix in gelatin into remaining ¼ cup water, liquid soap, and cornstarch mixture. Add kool aid for color and aroma. Put in fridge for 12 hours before using.

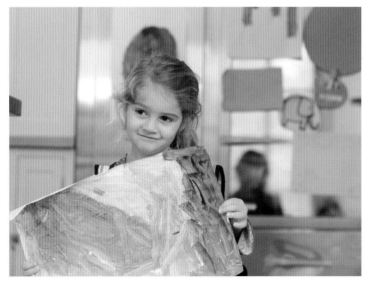

Salt and Finger Paint Recipe

2 cup flour
2 tsp salt
3 cups cold water
2 cups hot water
food coloring

Add salt to flour in saucepan. Pour in cold water gradually and beat with egg beater until smooth. Add hot water and boil mixture until glossy. Mix in food coloring and cool before using.

Water Color Paint

This needs to be made ahead.

1 tbsp white vinegar

1 tbsp baking soda

1 tbsp cornstarch

¼ tsp glycerin

Food coloring

Mix vinegar and baking soda in bowl. When mixture stops bubbling add cornstarch and glycerin. Mix well. Add colors and put in small containers to store in fridge.

Oatmeal Playdough

1 part flour

1 part water

2 part oatmeal

Combine, mix, knead until smooth. Store in fridge.

234

GLOSSARY

Aggressive Self: The strong sense of self that allows a human to struggle through day to day developmental challenges including basic survival.

Attachment: The process of developing a caring relationship between a baby and primary adult. The goal of the attachment process is to model a caring, secure, and trusting experience for a child to replicate in relationships in later life.

Body Rhythms: The development of regular eating, sleeping, and elimination patterns.

Circles of Communication: A concept developed by Stanley Greenspan, which advocates that an adult tunes into a child by following his special interests, taking a child's ideas one step further, through gestures and words, and allowing a child to close the circle when he is ready.

Cognitive Development: The development of thinking, reasoning, morality, and language skills.

Controlling Impulses: The ability to identify a desire and to intentionally control behavior.

Developmental Continuum: Understanding a child's development as a continuous process following a very individual trajectory or path.

Emotion Coaching: A parenting approach developed by John Gottman to help parents support young children as they develop an understanding of their emotions.

Family System: The make up of a family and their bi-directional or give and take interactions.

Floor Time: A technique developed by Stanley Greenspan as an engaged, warm, respectful way of tuning into children.

Intentional Toddler: The emergence of a toddler's desire to do things herself.

235

Magical Thinking: The mix of fantasy and reality; the sense that wishing something makes it happen. This develops in toddlerhood and continues into preschool.

Neurons: The cells of the nervous system. Neuron development is a complex communication highway that starts in the embryo and continues through young adulthood making brain connections thoughout development.

ProSocial Behavior: The development of a toddler as she internalizes rules of social behavior including sympathy, sharing, and helping others.

Scaffolding: The practice of modeling that a parent or caring adult can provide for a child as she learns a new skill.

Self Conscious Toddler: The development of a toddler's ability to see how others see him.

Self Regulation: The ability of a toddler to develop the capacity to recognize and adjust both feelings and behaviors as he develops more autonomy.

Separation Anxiety: A child's reaction to unfamiliar faces with frightened expression or other distress; this occurs around 9 months, consistent with memory development, and is consistent across cultures.

Shared Meanings: As children gain practice with language, they communicate ideas with words that include emotional themes that have connections with others around them.

Temperament: Individual characteristics of response including persistence, emotional mood regulation, and flexibility. These qualities are not fixed at birth but develop quite early and help shape the patterns of a child's later development.

Toddlerhood: The period beginning in the second year of a baby's life. It is marked by physical transformation including vigorous crawling, pulling up, walking, and the emergence of language and concrete thought.

INDEX

A

activity levels, 7
adaptability, 4–5
airplane travel, 34, 35, 94–95, 152
allergies
  Benadryl, 46
  and birthday parties, 162–63
  diet without dairy, 162
  EpiPen, 46–47, 163
  food labels, 47
  frozen treats, 163
  hidden ingredients, 47
  most allergic foods, 46
  restrictions, 162
  and school, 106, 163
  sweet alternatives, 107
  testing for, 107
  websites, 106
art, 176–77, 185
attention spans, 4

B

babysitters, 65
baths, 26, 86, 89
bedtime. *See also* sleep
  challenges, 86–87, 144–45
  Daylight Savings Time, 144
  drinks, 145
  frustrations, 85, 86, 144–45
  nightmares, 145
  reading, 27
  sleep routines, 27, 86
behavior problems, 212–13
biting, 111
books. *See also* reading
  about feelings, 175, 211
  about food, 103, 164
  about gardening, 164–65
  for and about traveling, 95, 152–53
  favorite reads, 173
  great toddler books, 114
  libraries, 57

  memory books, 61
  during mother's pregnancy, 67
  nightime, 87
  and outings, 70
  seasonal, 173
  story lines, 114
  story times, 57, 114
  toddler options, 115
  and toilet training, 194, 195, 197, 198
bottles, 90–91, 100–101, 149
brains and learning, 108, 166–67

C

calcium requirements, 100
The Carrot Seed (Krauss), 165
car trips, 34, 152–53
cleanup times, 222–23
climbing, 15, 29, 75, 135
clinging, 79, 125
cognitive development, 12–13, 72–73, 132–33
communication, 20–21, 80–81, 140–41

computer time, 220
coordination and motor abilities, 134
Counting Kisses (Katz), 114
creative arts, 176–77
cribs, 144
cuddling, 27

D
dads, 65, 119, 138
dancing, 113, 176–77
day care and preschools
    evaluating, 62, 122, 184–85
    and illnesses, 151
    preparing for, 182–83
    primary teachers, 127
    school lunches, 155
    staff, 183, 184–85
    and toilet training, 203
    transitions, 127, 182
dental care tips, 30, 91, 148–49
dentists, 30–31, 90–91, 148–49
diapers, 202–3
Diary of a Worm (Cronin), 164
doctor visits, 32–33, 92–93, 150–51, 202
drawing, 176
DVDs, 221

E
ear infections, 150
Early Intervention, 151
emotional development and awareness, 16–17, 76–77, 136–37
emotion coaching, 16, 76, 121, 136, 208–9, 215
emotions
aggression, 209
    anger, 17, 77, 137
    and communicating, 207–9
    confidence, 142–43
    developing pride, 82
    jealousy, 189
    need for closeness, 83
    normal aggression, 209
    and ongoing interactions, 136
    overstimulation, 180–81
    parents' understanding of, 206–7
    sadness, 17, 77, 137
    shame, 142
expressive language, 21

F
falling down, 74–75, 93
family. *See also* siblings
    birth order, 10–11

family time, 189
    importance of, 178–79
    mealtimes, 44–45, 104–5, 160–61
    rituals, 44–45, 226–27
farmers' markets, 165
Fast Food (Freymann and Elffers), 164
fears, 5
food and eating. *See also* allergies,
    snacks
    cooking together, 156
    cultural differences, 43, 97
    dining out, 43, 157
    eating habits, 6, 42–43
    favorite foods, 154–55
    food dumping, 43
    food power struggles, 38–39, 96, 98
    fruity shake recipe, 103
    grazing, 41
    high chairs, booster seats and table
        and chair sets, 39, 99
    holiday meal challenges, 161
    hunger strikes, 102–3
    importance of, 40–41
    introducing new foods, 99
    mealtime challenges, 36
    mealtime manners, 156–57
    mealtimes, 36–37, 44–45, 96–97, 104–5, 154–55, 160–61
    messy eating, 37, 97
    muffin tins, 159
    and obesity, 154
    online nutrition presentations, 101
    packing school lunches, 155
    picky eaters, 101, 158–59
    popular toddler foods, 96
    portions, 37, 99
    preventing eating disorders, 158–59
    preventing health problems, 154
    self-feeding struggles, 37
    and sleep, 40
    table food, 38–39
    utensils, 42, 96, 157
food labels, 47
Freight Train (Crews), 114
friendships, 68–69, 128–29, 178–79, 190–91

G
gardening, 164–65
gestures, 79
good-byes, 64, 65, 126–27, 187
Gottman, John, 16
grandparents, 61, 121, 138, 179
Grandpa's Garden (Kilroy), 164
Greenspan, Stanley, 59
group settings
    activities, 62, 122–23, 184–85
        imitating, 69, 122–23
        observing, 19, 62–63
growth charts, 40
guidelines, age-appropriate, 204–5
gym classes, 51, 71

H
hand-eye coordination, 72
hand washing, 92–93, 193
Happy Egg (Krauss), 114

head injuries, 33
health plan and medical history, 150
hitting, 23

I

I Can Eat a Rainbow (Karmel), 164
imitating behaviors, 69, 109, 122–23
independence
   autonomy, 133
   and choices, 85, 159
   dressing, 84
   eating, 96, 159
   growth of, 7
   leaving the house, 84
   and support, 84–85

J

Jamberry (book), 103

L

language development, 20–21, 80–81, 129, 140–41

M

manners, 69, 129, 156–57, 161
media exposure, 220–21
milestones
   cognitive development, 12–13
   language, 80, 140
   physical development, 14, 74, 134, 151
   self-esteem, 82
   social development, 18, 78–79
moist wipes, 201
moods, 2–3, 5, 208
moral development, 111
muscle control, 75
music, 80, 113, 176–77

N

Napping House (Wood), 114
naps, 6, 26, 87, 144, 174, 192

O

outings and excursions
   aquariums, 70
   beaches, 70, 71
   farms and orchards, 70
   getting out, 19
   museums, 70, 180
   open spaces, 71
   parks, 70
   shopping, 63
   socialization, 63
   transition time, 25
   zoos, 70, 169
overstimulation, 63, 180–81

P

pacifiers, 90–91, 149
parents
   acknowledging positive behavior, 142
   attitudes, 8–9
   and consistency, 73, 213

and emotions, 8–9
encouraging creativity, 176
examining own childhoods, 214–15
and grandparents, 121
importance of self-care, 217
journaling, 214
keeping feelings in check, 214–15
mini getaways, 217
and play, 118–19, 174–75
public parenting, 209
relationships with partners, 218–19
and short breaks, 125
staying healthy, 151
time alone with each child, 227
time for yourself, 216–17
time managment, 224–25
toilet training, 194–95
transition to parenting, 10–11
persistence, 4–5
physical development, 14–15, 74–75
playdates, 19, 50, 60, 68–69, 123, 128–29
playing. *See also* toys
with adults, 58–59, 118–19, 174–75

bully behavior, 190
conflicts, 191
creating play setups, 110
dramatic play, 167, 168–69
floor time, 59, 98–99, 117
focused playtime, 117
gender differences and awareness, 59, 167–69, 175
gender identification, 119
goals for playtime, 116
grabbing, 50, 60, 68, 125
helping toddlers play, 124–25
imaginary play, 113, 169

241

importance of, 48–49
and messes, 113
and observing, 49
and older toddlers, 166–67
outside, 109
parallel play, 110–11
props, 81, 168–69
and relaxing, 124
scaffolding, 49
with siblings, 51, 117
solitary play, 49, 50–51
solving problems, 166–67
stages, 48
story games, 153
themes, 168
toddler connections, 110–11
play spaces, 54–55

potty training. *See* toilet training
potty types, 200
pregnancy and toddlers, 66–67, 130–31
preschools. *See* day care and preschools
problem-solving and modeling, 118
public toilets, 196

R
reading. *See also* books
at bedtime, 27
and books, 56–57
library, 57, 173, 221
real-life connections, 115
spaces for, 172
story times, 57, 221
receptive language, 21
recognition of self, 23
regularity and activity, 6–7
relaxing and slowing down, 180–81
rewards, 198–99
roughhousing, 58, 116

S
safety issues
bathrooms, 93
bath water, 89
bikes, 146
car seats and seatbelts, 28, 88
climbing, 15, 29
floor mats, 93
grocery carts, 29, 88
infant/toddler CPR, 146
matches and lighters, 89
medicines and vitamins, 89
outlet covers, 89, 93
poison control, 89
pools, 146
at preschool and day care, 147
safe environments, 3, 213
safety gates, 89, 135
shopping carts, 88
smoke alarms, 89
strollers, 28, 88
swimming classes, 146
toilets and buckets, 146
toys, 55

tub faucets, 93
walking, xii–1, 14–15
water heaters, 89
water safety, 146
window guards, 89
schedules and routines, 24–25, 84–85, 86
self-esteem, 22–23, 82–83, 143
separation anxiety, 64–65, 84, 126–27, 138–39, 186–87
shoes, 15
siblings
introducing a new baby in the family, 66–67, 188–89
mealtimes, 104–5
older children, 11
playing, 51, 117
relationships, 61
social connections, 120, 139, 178
sick toddlers, 32, 92–93, 148, 203
sippy cups, 42, 101, 148
sleep, 6–7, 26–27, 40, 86–87, 144–45. *See also* bedtime
Sleep in the Jeep (Apple), 114
snacks
choices, 36
and comfort, 98
healthy, 155, 159
before mealtimes, 38, 97
outings, 70
tooth decay, 148
traveling, 95
social connections, 120–21, 179
social skills and development
and dads, 138
friendships, 68
and grandparents, 138
group settings, 62
interactions, 18–19
learning, 60–63
meeting new adults, 79, 139
milestones, 78–79
observing, 62
other toddlers, 60
play behavior, 60

T
technology advances, 220
teeth, 30–31, 148–49
telephones, 21

television, 220–21
temperaments, 2–3, 6, 8, 78–79, 136–37, 208
temper tantrums, 210–13
thumb sucking, 149
toddlerhood, xii–1
toilet inserts, 200
toilet training, 192–203
Toolbox (diPaola), 114
toothaches, 31, 148
toothbrushing, 30, 91
toys
blocks, 13, 73, 170–71
boxes, 15, 171
cleaning, 53, 223
doctor kits, 150
flexible toys, 170–71
gender differences, 59

INDEX

good young toddler toys, 52

homemade, 171

importance of, 52–53

must-haves for play, 112

for older toddlers, 170

for painting and coloring, 53

for pouring and dumping, 53, 133

preferences, 59

puzzles, 13, 73, 132, 170

recycling, 170

riding toys, 53

rotating, 222

storage and organizing, 54–55, 222–23

wagons, 171

traveling

airplanes, 34, 35, 94–95, 152

car trips, 34, 152–53

entertainment, 34, 95

with older toddlers, 152–53

packing tips, 35, 94, 95

preparing for long trips, 152

schedules and routines, 85, 94–95

and toilet training, 200

by train, 152

trust, 126

U

underwear, 202–3

V

The Very Hungry Caterpillar (book), 103

vitamin supplements, 154

W

walking, xii–1, 14–15

water, drinking, 41

We Are Going on a Bear Hunt (Rosen and Oxenbury), 114

Where's My Teddy (Alborough), 114

Y

Yummy Yucky (Patricelli), 164

INDEX